NAPOLEON HILL'S SECRET

NAPOLEON HILL'S SECRET

DON M. GREEN
Executive Director
Napoleon Hill Foundation

Humanix Books
www.humanixbooks.com

Humanix Books

NAPOLEON HILL'S SECRET by Don M. Green
Copyright © 2023 by Napoleon Hill Foundation
All rights reserved

Humanix Books, P.O. Box 20989, West Palm Beach, FL 33416, USA
www.humanixbooks.com | info@humanixbooks.com

Humanix Books is a division of Humanix Publishing, LLC. Its trademark, consisting
of the words "Humanix Books," is registered in the U.S. Patent and Trademark Office
and in other countries.

ISBN: 9-781-63006-243-9 (Hardcover)
ISBN: 9-781-63006-244-6 (E-book)

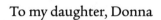

To my daughter, Donna

Contents

Introduction

You can't have everything in life.

However, you can have everything you really want.

Sound impossible? It isn't. Is there a trick to it? No, no tricks. But there is a method, and I'm going to show you how it works. It's not an overnight technique. You'll have to invest time and energy, and you won't have everything you want tomorrow. There aren't three simple steps to happiness. On the other hand, no prescription is required, no coupons need to be redeemed, and no one will call on you at home.

Just what do you want, anyway?

Wealth? Happiness? Love? Authority? Respect? Fame? Independence?

They can be yours.

If they are what you really want.

Do you know what you really want?

The key to your answer will lie in discovering how you define success, and then developing a plan for creating that success and following through on it.

THINK AND GROW RICH

Think and Grow Rich was written by Napoleon Hill in 1937. In the midst of the Great Depression, it became an immediate national bestseller. It still continues to influence hundreds of thousands of new readers, maybe millions, every year. A *USA Today* survey of business leaders ranked it among the top ten inspirational works of all time.

One of the appeals of *Think and Grow Rich* lies in its ability to help you understand yourself and what you want out of life. As one of the first popular books to apply the ideas of modern psychology to everyday life, despite the catchy title, the book doesn't assume to know what your definition of "rich" is, only to help you make that idea real. Countless people have written testimonials to its power. Many have told me it's the most important book they read, after only the Bible.

Think and Grow Rich was based on a massive earlier work by Napoleon Hill called *Law of Success*, published in 1928. This was another national bestseller, but it was simply too expensive for most people in Depression-era America. The *Law of Success*, in turn, grew out of a conversation that Napoleon Hill had with the industrialist Andrew Carnegie. A novice reporter, Hill had blithely asked Carnegie what made people successful. Carnegie turned things around and asked Hill if the young man could figure out the answer to that question himself.

Hill spent twenty years studying successful people in many walks of life. He interviewed the likes of Thomas Edison and Woodrow Wilson, Henry Ford, and Luther

Burbank, trying to find out what distinguished them from ordinary folk. He also studied great figures of history and became acquainted with the work of leaders of the human potential movement such as William James and Émile Coué.

He distilled all that he discovered into *The Law of Success* and then even further into the powerful *Think and Grow Rich*. Though times have changed, human nature has not, and the ideas in those two books are as practical and as useful as they ever have been.

In this book, I hope to present helpful suggestions and guidance as to how to apply the principles in these two books. Realizing what you want and following through on a concrete plan for making it happen are the keys to getting what this book promises you. Being able to do this will require some honest soul-searching on your part. You'll probably have to confront some uncomfortable truths about your life. You'll certainly have to work hard. You'll likely have to give up some things that are familiar, some of which you may miss for a while. Others you'll probably be very happy to get rid of.

All of these changes will begin in one place: your mind.

MENTAL POWER

One of the most liberating and frightening phrases that Napoleon Hill coined is, "Whatever the mind can conceive and believe, it can achieve."

It's liberating because it tells you that anything is possible as long as you can work out a plan for attaining it and then follow through on that plan with conviction. Note an important caveat there: you must be able to come up with the plan. A world-changing goal is possible with a plan; even the most modest ambition won't come true without one.

> **Unless you assign your mind a task, it may end up actually creating problems for you.**

It's frightening because you have to ask yourself what happens if you don't actively conceive of a plan. The answer is—nothing you want. Your life will be patternless. You won't be doing much more than responding to one problem after another, never getting a chance to do what you want to do. Does this sound familiar already? Worse, unless you assign your mind a task, it may end up actually creating problems for you. Remember, whatever you can conceive and believe, you can achieve. If your mind is occupied with worrying, it's going to create more things to worry about. It will conceive, believe, and achieve things you don't want.

How exactly does this power of your mind work? The human mind—your mind—is something unique in the known universe. While many life forms have some kind of consciousness, the human mind alone is capable of dreaming and long-term planning. Other creatures may build, as beavers do, or use strategy to complete tasks, the way wolves do when they hunt in a pack. But humans alone can think in terms of next week, next month, or next year. We have the ability to envision another time, imagine what it might be like, and determine what we need to do to prepare for that time.

Because we do this kind of planning automatically, we sometimes take it for granted. But we do it every time we undertake a task. We do tasks because we anticipate a need of some sort, whether for food, shelter, or retirement money.

Sometimes, we hope for things without really planning for them. We all know what it's like to fantasize about how life would be if we got a big raise, published that

Your mind is the only thing you can truly call your own.

novel to great acclaim, or bought a vacation home. When we dream like this, we gloss over the details of how we get there—or imagine shortcuts like our boss's moving to Borneo, a burst of creativity over a rainy weekend, or a wise stock market investment.

Those little shortcuts are why we don't have those things we dream about, no matter how much we dream about them. We aren't using both powers of the mind together. We can imagine something, but we don't plan for it to become real. In essence, this book will teach you to link the powers of your mind and put them to work.

RECLAIMING YOUR OWN

Napoleon Hill was fond of saying that your mind is the only thing you can truly call your own. Money and property can be lost or taken from you. Loved ones can die or leave you. You can be imprisoned so that even your life itself isn't really yours. But your mind is something that can always be yours. You can choose both what it thinks about and how it thinks.

However, most people don't exercise this fundamental right.

Your first reaction to this statement is probably to scoff. After all, you don't live in a totalitarian state; you aren't a member of a cult. You know you make your own decisions all the time—some of them pretty darn good. And even when you do have to do something you don't want to do, you know it and aren't happy about it.

But let me ask you this: Why, then, are you reading this book?

It's because you don't have what you want most in life.

If you truly had full control of your own mind, you would have what you wanted or be so obviously on the road to it that you wouldn't be seeking help. The truth is, you haven't begun to control your mind and your thoughts.

Let me give you a little list of things that would be happening to you if you had full control of your thoughts:

1. Every day, you would be doing something that brought you closer to your goal.
2. Every time you had to do something you didn't want to do, you'd be finding a way to make it pay off for yourself.
3. Every time you got bad news, you'd be finding good news along with it.
4. Every person around you would be a source of inspiration.

Do these things sound impossible? They're not, and this book can teach you how to make all of these things happen.

The first step is to realize that you can't control everything that happens to you in life. The company you work for may be sold, the economy may change, accidents may happen, other people's goals and needs might take new turns, illness may arise, and so on. You can't prevent these things from happening, even though they throw a monkey wrench into your plans for your own life.

What you can control is the manner in which you react to them. They can be disasters that paralyze your decision-making, fill you with rage, awaken your worst fears, or sink you into depression. Or, they can serve as challenges, opportunities, and wake-up calls. You can decide to take control of the situation you're in and use your mental powers to find a way to turn the bad news into an advantage.

Taking charge of your life this way depends completely on taking charge of your mind. And since you're the only one with that power, no one else is going to do it for you.

WHAT LIES AHEAD

Let me briefly outline what you're going to learn from this book and how it will help you.

Being Positive

The key technique for controlling your thoughts is to learn to maintain a Positive Mental Attitude, or PMA. PMA is a term that Napoleon Hill used, which has since entered into the general vocabulary of inspirational writing. You'll find it, or the ideas it expresses, in the works of many leading writers, including Og Mandino, Anthony Robbins, Zig Ziglar, and Susan Jeffers.

Napoleon Hill defined PMA as a confident, honest, constructive state of mind that you create and maintain by methods of your own choosing. Hill's longtime associate W. Clement Stone added, "A Positive Mental Attitude is the right honest thought, action, or reaction to a given situation or set of circumstances."

I'll provide you with a whole list of exercises for developing and maintaining PMA. PMA will give you the mental control you need to pursue your objective, along with emotional clarity, increased planning ability, dogged persistence, and the joy of going the extra mile.

Thinking in Sync

Maybe there are people who get exactly what they want out of life without help from anybody else—people who always have every resource they need, all the knowledge they require, and all the time in the world, all by themselves—but I have no idea who they are.

You're going to need help, and you can get it through an arrangement that Napoleon Hill called the *Master Mind*. It's a way of getting a special group of people—maybe two, maybe twenty—working toward the same goal. They all share their expertise, time, dedication, and anything else they can bring to the table. You can start a group like this and use it to help you achieve your goal.

Understanding What You Want

As this introduction has repeatedly emphasized, you can't have everything, but you can have what you want. The trick is discovering just what it is that you want from life. You can't proceed on any front until you know this for certain. Napoleon Hill often said, "First, know what you want."

One reason the PMA concept precedes the one on defining your major purpose in this book is that, with PMA, you'll have the freedom to cast off any negative ideas about what you're capable of doing. Maybe you'll want to make big changes in your life; PMA will help you see that those changes are possible. Maybe you'll have to give up some old ideas about what you are and aren't able to accomplish. You can do exactly that.

And even if you already know precisely what you want to accomplish, you'll find that this principle illuminates the specifics that have eluded you so far and the roadblocks in your way. That knowledge will be essential to moving on to the next concept.

Making Your Plan

Even the clearest goal will lie forever in the distance unless you know how and when you're going to reach it. You absolutely must have a plan for getting what you want out of life, and that plan must be loaded with specifics.

A central idea in this book is that *you* control your plan: it doesn't control you. You don't need to worry about trapping yourself in the pursuit of something that ceases to matter to you or finding yourself making sacrifices that render your ultimate goal worthless. Remember, this entire process is about finding success as you define it.

Starting the Fire

With your definition of success complete, you'll need to begin fueling your determination to achieve it. The most powerful source of energy for your work ahead is your own enthusiasm for what you want. Properly used, enthusiasm will be a dynamo that will propel you forward and make the things you want happen.

> **The most powerful source of energy for your work ahead is your own enthusiasm for what you want.**

Enthusiasm is something you can create in yourself. It's easiest to create when you're working for something you desire, but you can also call upon it when you're facing tasks that seem incredibly trivial or endless. It's strongly tied to PMA, and the two forces together amplify each other in a never-ending circle.

Once you learn to harness this chain reaction, you'll find you possess incredible reserves of energy. You'll be able to infect other people with that energy—and they'll appreciate you for it. You can actually develop mental triggers that unleash a burst of enthusiasm when you most need it, so that no matter how dull or unpleasant an obstacle you confront, you'll be able to tackle it and make progress.

Surviving Disappointment

You're going to take some knocks as you pursue your definite major purpose. There is absolutely no way to avoid setbacks and reversals. The world isn't going to hand you what you want just because you ask for it; the world isn't made that way.

What separates successful people from failures is how they respond to bad news. Once again, PMA will be crucial to your efforts, but forget any idea that it will simply allow you to overlook the things you don't want to acknowledge. It will require you to look them full in the face, understand them, and then do something about whatever caused them.

You'll also find out how to look back at disappointments you've already experienced and understand just how they happened to you. Some of them may have been your fault, and you'll have to accept that truth

> **What separates successful people from failures is how they respond to bad news.**

and decide how to prevent those disappointments from happening again. Some of them may have been completely beyond your control. Even so, it will be crucial for you to discover whether they are still affecting the way you live your life and then to decide what to do about that.

Equally important will be recognizing that every negative thing that has ever happened to you can be turned into something positive. That may seem impossible from where you sit today, but you can extract something good and worthwhile from every disappointment you've faced. Once you've learned to do that, you'll gain enormous power over your life.

Staying the Course

Sometimes, we get bogged down in details. There are so many different things that need to be done—dull, repetitive tasks that offer almost no short-term or long-term gratification. No one's life offers one triumphant victory after another, and it's easy to become distracted by things that give us at least a momentary setback or diversion.

Self-discipline is the key to making sure that you keep working toward your goals and don't become stuck in a rut. You can train yourself to make daily progress—progress that you can see and recognize—toward the things you want. Just as important, you'll find that self-discipline will be another tool you can use when you face down disappointment—or when you decide to expand your ambitions and strive for even more than you first believed possible.

> **Self-discipline is the key to making sure that you keep working toward your goals.**

Don't think that this will mean becoming a mindless robot. Self-discipline isn't so much about denial as about pursuing your goals. Self-discipline can liberate you, excite you, and give you a feeling of control, not only over yourself but also over every aspect of your life.

Taking Some Risks

You're going to have to make yourself vulnerable if you want success. Even if security is a key element in how you define happiness, you're going to have to take some chances and make changes in your life that could discourage or even frighten you. You may have to put some money on the line, give up a comfortable situation, or alter the dynamics of relationships that are part of how you define yourself.

To do this, you'll need something Napoleon Hill called *applied faith*. This is the willingness to act on the assumption that things will turn out the way you want while at the same time doing everything you can to make that result possible. Applied faith isn't the same as religious faith, though if you have it, you'll probably see some similarities. Applied faith is finding the courage to act on the belief that your goals are worthy and attainable.

> **Applied faith gives you the strength to undertake challenges you may have avoided in the past.**

Applied faith gives you the strength to undertake challenges you may have avoided in the past. It lets you decide that past mistakes and failures don't have to be repeated. Applied faith frees you to look at something that is already good, see how it could be better, and then make it better. Acting on applied faith can be intimidating, but every time you do it, you'll experience a sense of satisfaction that will be worth any fear that you had to face down.

Thinking Big and Small

From the moment you began trying to define your goal, you were drawing on your imagination—the creative power of your mind. Your imagination is always active, but it isn't always doing what you want. You can change that.

It's almost impossible to overstate just what you can accomplish with imagination as your ally. You can discover opportunities, build motivation, and convey your excitement about your objectives to the people you work with or the people you love. But you can also solve little problems, eliminate distractions, and discover entirely new paths to getting what you want.

You can use many different techniques to inspire your imagination and train it to support you. Every time you put your imagination to work, it will become stronger, more flexible, and more creative. Most of these techniques can be applied anytime and anywhere, and you can easily teach them to other people. When you do that, you'll surround yourself with an amazing wealth of creativity and insight that you'll be able to draw on again and again as you advance toward your major purpose.

Putting the World on a String

At the risk of sounding like a popular magazine article, I promise that you can become more influential by making yourself a compelling, inspiring person whom people want to know. I'm talking about improving your personality. You can have a vision of yourself as a confident person who projects resolve, wins cooperation, demonstrates reliability, and is a pleasure to be around. There are proven, reliable, and authentic ways to express these aspects of yourself, and you can master every one.

One immediate benefit is that you'll build self-respect. You'll gain faith in what you're trying to do and be able to express that faith. And you'll also find that you'll start gaining more allies in your quest. People will want to help you because they'll take pleasure in seeing you succeed. It will be an astounding transformation that will immediately increase the pleasure you get out of life.

> **Exceeding other people's expectations is incredibly rewarding.**

Living a Value-Added Life

Napoleon Hill called this "going the extra mile." It means doing more than you're expected to do in a pleasant manner. It doesn't mean being a doormat or a wimp. The value-added life is a way of living and working that can become part of every relationship you have for the rest of your life.

Exceeding other people's expectations is incredibly rewarding. You'll constantly reinforce your sense of self-confidence. You'll be proud of the work you do—even if you don't enjoy it some of the time. You'll also discover that people are inspired to return your good deeds in kind, especially the people who are most likely to be able to help you reach your goal.

> **You'll be happy with yourself, which is one of the most valuable states of being.**

Yes, inevitably, some people will take advantage of this type of living. However, rest assured that if you offer those people more than they offer you, you'll be preparing yourself to move on and away from them sooner than if you resent them and begrudge them every moment of your work. In the meantime, you'll be happy with yourself, which is one of the most valuable states of being.

Thinking Like a Boss

If you want to take control of all the things in your life, you'll need to think and act like you're the person in charge. This has to happen long before you achieve your goal, and it has to apply to things large and small. It's called "showing initiative."

Initiative requires recognizing a goal, making a plan, and following through. Imagine what would happen if you were taking positive action in every one of your re-

Showing initiative makes you shine in a world full of people who are just getting by. lationships at home and at work, taking concrete steps to pursue your mutual goals, and demonstrating that you can accomplish what you set out to do. You'd become more valuable in that relationship, admired, and trusted. You'd gain a bigger voice in what was happening and going to happen.

Initiative can become a thrilling, exciting habit. It can begin in the smallest details of the things you do and grow quickly to encompass everything you're involved in. It empowers you, even in situations where you're working for someone else. Showing initiative makes you shine in a world full of people who are just getting by. And, it will give you the satisfaction of accomplishing things every day.

Becoming Mentally Fit

Like your body, your mind can become efficient and toned, capable of hard work with great stamina. You'll need twin mental abilities for this to happen: accurate thinking and controlled attention.

Accurate thinking is the ability to sort things out, set priorities, and recognize fact from fiction, as well as to know when you don't have enough information to make that distinction. Controlled attention means having the willpower to avoid distractions. The two quali- ties are closely related, and they also have a strong relationship to your ability to harness your imagination.

> Having mental fitness means you are in charge of your life.

Mental fitness will have an impact on almost every aspect of what you're learning from this book because it gives you self-discipline, organizes your initiative, and controls your enthusiasm. Most important, though, it's part of being in control of how you think and thus who you are. Having mental fitness means *you* are in charge of your life.

Creating Harmony

Attaining your major definite purpose depends entirely on you. However—and this is a big "however"—having the life you want is almost impossible without some cooperation from other people. Your journey will be smoother, faster, and more enjoyable when you understand how to get people to help you.

The basis of cooperation is the intersection of personal interests. While it might seem that any two or more people who have a common goal would naturally work together, this often doesn't happen. Issues such as personality conflicts, disagreements about methods, and lack of a common frame of reference often sabotage many potential cooperative relationships.

This doesn't have to happen to you. You can become a person who creates the kind of harmony that facilitates cooperation. You have to be deliberate and painstaking about it, and you need many of the skills you'll have learned in earlier chapters to do it effectively: imagination, enthusiasm, clear thinking, and a winning personality. But if you combine all these qualities in the pursuit of harmony, you can enlist many people in the quest for your goal.

Managing Your Resources

For most of us, time and money always seem to be in short supply, and there are hordes of people making demands on them. You can't always increase your supply of either, but if you pay close attention to how your time and money are spent and saved, you'll find that it seems as if you have more of both.

Many simple techniques can give you real control over how you spend time and money. Being aware of your own unconscious ideas about how to use time and money is the first step toward initiating changes in the way you deal with them.

Making habits of good time and money management will take an enormous burden off your shoulders, even when it seems that all the money and time you have are going to other people. If you learn to control the flow of these resources in your life, you gain important power. The sooner you begin asserting some authority over time and money, the more you'll find is available for yourself.

Living Smart

Staying healthy is essential to being able to pursue and enjoy whatever you want most in life. Most of us, though, don't explicitly think of health when we imagine where we want to be. As a consequence, we ignore our health or decide that taking care of our minds and bodies is something we can sacrifice in the pursuit of our goals.

> You need a sound body and a sound mind to get where you want to be.

It's a big mistake. You need a sound body and a sound mind to get where you want to be. Forget about enjoying the fruits of your labor: you'll drop in your tracks if you treat yourself like an overworked farm animal. You'll have to make clear decisions about taking care of yourself if you ever want to be successful.

Making the Great Connection

Finally, you're going to need to put all the ideas you've learned in this book together. Along the way, you'll have seen how they're related, but the glue that binds them all into a coherent philosophy is an amazing idea about how the world and the universe work. I'm not going to say much about this idea here, partly because I'd like you to be looking for the connections yourself and partly because it will all make so much more sense to you when you've read each of the chapters and started to apply them in your own life. There is more to this book and the ideas of Napoleon Hill than reading alone can reveal to you.

You'll need some experience putting them into practice to fully appreciate what you can do to change your life.

Taking the Plunge

Are you ready to have what you want most in life? I'm sure you are.

Action is absolutely essential. But let me offer you a word of caution.

It will never be enough to just read this book. You're going to have to act. You're going to have to follow all the little suggestions—and the big ones—and incorporate them into your life. Action is absolutely essential.

And that action will have consequences.

Your life is going to change. You won't feel like the same person anymore. Other people will notice that you've changed. They'll change the way they react to you, and their ideas about who you are and what you can do will change as well.

Nothing will ever be the same.

But then, that's part of what you wanted, isn't it?

Let's get started!

Chapter 1

Being Positive

"A positive mental attitude is the foundation of all success, and to be maintained, the mind must be fed with positive thoughts."

—Napoleon Hill

Let's pretend for a moment that you're in trouble. You stand on the street in a big city, owning nothing more than the clothes you're wearing. Your wallet is empty. You have no job, no home. There are no friends or family to help you. What do you do?

It's a bewildering predicament, isn't it? Do you look for work, for shelter? Do you try to find some kind of assistance? Do you beg from passersby? What is going to happen to you? You have nothing to call your own but the clothes on your back.

Or do you?

You bet you do. You have the most valuable possession in the world.

Your mind.

I'm not talking about skills you have learned like reading and writing, knowledge of interstate commerce law, or how to change the oil in your car. These things are useless to you, unless you first recognize that you still have an incredible power: you alone can control how and what you're thinking. If you do control your thinking, you'll be able to cope with the situation you're in. If you don't take hold of yourself and your thoughts, you're finished. Because if you find yourself broke and alone, your first reaction is likely to be a mixture of fear, despair, and panic. That's only human.

If you have control of your mind, you won't let all those negative emotions push you over the edge. You'll realize that you need to make a plan and do something fast. You'll know that you still have the ability and the freedom to do something, to make choices and decisions. And in that moment of knowing that you have the power of your mind, you'll understand that you can change the circumstances you're in.

Your mental attitude makes all the difference in the world between whether things get better or worse. And even in great situations, your mental attitude still determines whether things get better or worse. Your mental attitude always determines what is going to happen to you in the long run.

DECIDING TO MAKE A DIFFERENCE

You'll need an attitude that says, *It can be done! I can do it!* And you need to think that way even if, at that very moment, you haven't got a clear idea of what needs to be done or how it can be accomplished. So much cynicism runs through our culture these days that it's easy to scoff at such a bare essentials description of a Positive Mental Attitude. PMA alone won't get you to your goal. You need many other skills to get someplace in this world. But not having a PMA is like trying to swim across a lake while tied to a tree on the shore: you'll be holding yourself back.

There's no such thing as a Neutral Mental Attitude. You either have a PMA or its opposite, a Negative Mental Attitude. Unfortunately for most of us, a Negative Mental Attitude is the default mode—unless we train ourselves otherwise. And a Negative Mental Attitude can take hold of you even if you don't wake up each morning and say, "Something's gonna go wrong today, and I'm only gonna make it worse."

How and why does a Negative Mental Attitude creep into your life?

For most of us, it begins when we're kids. Children have a natural curiosity about the world, which is great because that's what impels us to learn. But during those impressionable, vulnerable years, two forces are at work that begin to curb our natural exuberance: our own bad experiences and the actions of the people around us.

There isn't a child born who doesn't take a few nasty falls while learning to walk; get bumped or cut exploring new territory; or discover that something cute and fun looking is also hot, sharp, or loud. It's an essential part of growing up that we discover the need to be cautious. After we've had a few scares, and we've inflicted a little terror on the grown-ups who discover us yelling our lungs out after getting a finger pinched in a door, we become suspicious of new things, new people, and new situations.

Grown-ups help reinforce this suspicion. No parent wants to find their baby playing with something sharp or sticking a pen into an electrical socket. We may not understand exactly what it is that Daddy is saying when he takes the fun thing away, but we do know that he's upset. And we don't like grown-ups to be upset.

You can't remedy these thoughts until you're conscious of them.

All this continues as we grow up. We retain enough spark to be interested in new things, but we still stumble, and along with our parents, we have friends, classmates, teachers, television, movies, and computers to remind us that life is full of peril. Once we're away from home and on our own—raising a family, building a career—the stakes are higher, and we're still bombarded with messages about how devastating failure can be.

The result is that we expect bad things. So, we create bad things.

A PMA is not an instant cure for all that ails you. It is, however, an essential first step in changing things that you're unhappy with. The following is a system for creating PMA in yourself.

IDENTIFY THE NEGATIVE

To begin, you need to recognize negative ideas you have about yourself. It's not pleasant to spend a lot of time dwelling on the negative, but you can't remedy these thoughts until you're conscious of them.

Get a notebook, preferably something small and portable because you'll want to have it with you. You'll use this notebook for other things as well, so choose something you find pleasant to work with. Make sure it has a cover, for the sake of your privacy. You'll want to feel safe being honest with yourself and not be worried about other people reading what you write.

Draw a line down the middle of the first page. On the left, begin making a list of what you consider your faults. If ugly words occur to you, write them down. It's important that you recognize your own thinking patterns. If you think "I'm fat," then write "fat," not "overweight." "Overweight" isn't the word that pops into your mind when you're mentally beating yourself up. You want to really understand your own negative thinking.

Don't spend more than five minutes working on the list right now. It's too easy to wallow in all these awful ideas about yourself. If you finish sooner, fine. Don't strain for negative ideas.

Next, go through the list and cross off any words that repeat the same ideas.

Now, on the right side of the line, write down the opposite idea to the negative thoughts you've discovered.

Spend the next day or two paying attention to how often you make a decision based on one of these negative ideas. Do you avoid offering a suggestion because *you* thought it, and *you're* not smart enough? Do you not start a project because you think you're lazy? Do you eat something you don't need because you already "know" you're fat?

My guess is you'll be overwhelmed by how often you're limiting yourself. You'll probably also discover that out of all the things on your list, there are two or three that pop up most often. You'll quickly see that a few negative ideas are at the root of many of the others.

You'll quickly see that a few negative ideas are at the root of many of the others.

Don't revel in the agony of these realizations because every time you think one of these terrible things about yourself, you're going to reinforce that idea. What you need to do immediately is begin replacing these negative impressions of yourself with positive ones.

TRANSFORMATION

Now that you're aware of your self-fulfilling negative ideas, it's time to begin purging them from the way you think.

This won't happen overnight, and it won't happen automatically. It will take conscious, regular, vigilant action from you. You're going to be altering mental habits that you've spent a long time acquiring. But it will be satisfying—very satisfying.

Tear your list out of your notebook. (It will feel good, getting rid of those hateful ideas.) Now, on a fresh page, for each one of your old, bad ideas, write down a short, concrete statement of its positive opposite. Make these statements emphatic. Don't be shy, cautious, or modest about them. Don't insert qualifying words or phrases like "sometimes" or "many people." Use the word "I" in every one of them. And state things positively, not negatively. Write "I am friendly," not "I don't hate anyone."

Be aggressive about these affirmations. Don't censor yourself by thinking that you aren't really smart. Don't settle for mildness. Write out something great that you would really like to be true about yourself. It won't take long for you to find out they are all true.

When your list is complete, choose the negative idea that pops up most often in your

When you take control of your mind by reining in negative thoughts, your positive side will be liberated.

thinking. For the next day, every time you find that idea has entered your thoughts, immediately and forcefully repeat the positive affirmation three times. Think it if you have to, but if you can say it, and say it determinedly, then say it!

The next day, add a second statement to your list of quick responses. By the third day, you'll have the hang of it, and you can begin using them all.

If you're like most people, you'll quickly find that the affirmations start popping into your head in another set of circumstances: when you act in complete accordance with the idea you're expressing.

Your capacity for positive thinking never dies. It can be overwhelmed by negative thinking, but it's there, eager to reassert itself. When you take control of your mind by reining in negative thoughts, your positive side will be liberated. While you're experiencing the excitement of a PMA, examine your life for ways in which you've already been acting, just as you imagined yourself being when you wrote your list of affirmations.

Most people find that there are already circumstances in which they are all the things on their list of affirmations. Are the situations all that different? Maybe you're a strong leader at church but find yourself unassertive at work. If you ironed out last year's fiscal budget for your department, perhaps that same eye for money and detail can be applied to managing the renovation of your house. You'll find a lot of possibilities pretty fast.

Don't be shy or hesitant about expressing these realizations you make about yourself. Yes, there may be some bumps. People may be surprised; they may resist the "new" you. You may have to feel your way a little. But remember, you're acting in a positive, admirable way, and even if things don't work out right the very first time, you'll still be better off than if you let yourself stay in the same old rut that had you so unsatisfied with your life that you bought a book on how to change it.

In a short time, you'll have completed your transformation. You'll have removed a bunch of limiting, negative ideas about yourself from your brain, and replaced them with exciting, positive, and true ideas.

THE PRICE OF ADMISSION

Have you ever seen the musical comedy, *How to Succeed in Business without Really Trying?* A vapid young man vaults up the corporate ladder with the help of an inane advice book. The show spoofs some popular ideas about personal motivation, and it's funny. Another play, Arthur Miller's *Death of a Salesman*, is a wrenching tragedy about the failure of the American Dream for a family who thought they were doing everything necessary to be rich and happy. Unfortunately, they were fooling themselves.

Both of these plays raise some good questions about the ability of the power of positive thinking alone to achieve your definite major purpose. They both make the following point: just because you want something and tell yourself that you can have it, doesn't mean you're going to get it.

PMA isn't about fantasizing. It isn't about deceiving yourself or other people. In fact, it requires accuracy and truthfulness with yourself and with other people. It's not about asking the universe for a small personal fortune and expecting to find it in your dresser drawer the next morning.

PMA is realistic, optimistic, and constructive. Each of those qualities depends on the other. Different people in the same circumstances, all using a PMA, may respond to those circumstances in very individual ways, but they will always be realistic, optimistic, and constructive. Only when you are all three of these things will your PMA really be able to do something for you.

Being *realistic* requires that you acknowledge your circumstances for what they are. At this point, you don't need to make any judgment about whether things are good or bad, but you can't be afraid to admit that things aren't what you want. *Optimism* means that you operate on the assumption that things can be improved, and being *constructive* means that you're willing to do something concrete about your circumstances.

PMA will only work if you plan on giving people something even more valuable for whatever you get from them. That "something valuable" may be goods, services, feelings, or knowledge, but it has to be real, and you have to give them more than you're getting from them.

That may sound like a paradox, but it's a requirement. It's the essence of being constructive because it means you're adding value to the world, making it a better place. You don't have to be like Mother Teresa, with a world-changing mission, but you must be prepared to improve things for the people you deal with.

What matters is that you're willing to give more than you get.

If you are, then a PMA will work for you.

GROWING PMA

Working with a PMA can be a heady experience. You'll value those moments when you feel yourself overcoming an obstacle or trying something you were afraid to do. Good things will happen to you, and those good times will be a great reinforcement to your new mental attitude.

However, there will be some bumps. Your PMA skills are still fresh and vulnerable, and things can happen that interrupt your progress. Somebody may make a passing comment that offends you. A realistic, optimistic, and constructive plan may be ambushed by a chance occurrence that blows you out of the water, leaving you wondering if you've been fooling yourself.

Here are two ways to strengthen your PMA so that you start off with some resilience. These exercises are great for bolstering your mental attitude, whether you're just beginning to use your PMA or you're a veteran user who has already known many triumphs. The nature of your mental attitude is something you choose, and you can do conscious, deliberate things to reinforce that attitude. Every time you make a choice about your attitude—even when there's nothing around to threaten it—you're strengthening your choice, underlining your decision.

Write a creed. A creed is a statement of beliefs. Many organizations have them because they give people something to turn to when they need help staying true to the goals and ideals that unite the organization's members. They might call it a mission statement or a slogan, but it does the same job. You can create the same kind of statement for yourself. Think of it as a promise to yourself about what you want and who you are.

Your creed should be written with the same kind of emphatic, concrete, positive language that you used for the positive affirmations earlier in this chapter. It doesn't have to be long or poetic: you just need to make sure it touches on all the issues you've decided to tackle. It doesn't have to be written in stone, either. You can adapt it as your life changes, inserting exciting new ideas about yourself.

After you've written out a creed that you like, put a copy of it somewhere you can read it over every day. You can tape it to the bathroom mirror, put it inside your

datebook, make it pop up on your computer, or just keep
it folded up in your wallet or purse. Anywhere will work
as long as you see it early in, each day. Take a moment
to read it each time you see it. You'll be reinforcing your
belief in your creed every time you read it. If you want to
put it all over your home or office, feel free.

But don't share it with anyone yet. There are two reasons for this. First, other people may not understand at
all why you're doing this. They might laugh, ask you embarrassing questions, or try to make you ashamed. You
don't owe anyone an explanation of what you're doing,
especially not someone who feels jealous that you know
exactly what your strong points are. Remember how you
felt before you discovered PMA? Wouldn't you be threatened by someone who seemed to have such a clear idea
of himself? For the moment, let your creed be a private
thing.

Second, give yourself time to discover things about
your creed and yourself. You might find that there are important aspects of your strengths that you've overlooked
and aren't reinforcing. You may decide to change the order of your sentences, to emphasize things differently, or
to state them in an even more concrete and powerful way.
Feel free to make changes like this a week after you've
written your creed or years down the line. The only person who has to be satisfied with it is you.

Before long, you'll find that you've memorized your
creed. Keep reading it daily anyway. Let the reading become a ritual, a signal to yourself that you believe in your
creed and that it's worthwhile. Make the reading a part of

your everyday life. Don't skip it on weekends or vacations either. Stay with it.

Once you've memorized your creed, it will be a super affirmation. It will be there in your mind in moments of crisis and decision-making. It will help you find your path over new territory and out of old problems. If your creed is playing in your mind when you're confronted by uncertainty or opportunity, it will clarify your thinking and help guide you to the choices that bring you closer to your goal.

The second exercise I call "fill in the blanks." When you're in the middle of fighting off a sense of looming doom, your mind will tend to keep covering the same ground over and over. You'll obsess about the bad things you're afraid are about to happen or will follow as a result of something bad that has already happened. This is not PMA.

The solution? Force yourself to concentrate on the good things that can happen.

I keep a little card with me, a sort of two-part essay question that I ask myself when I need to give PMA a boost. It reads like this:

1. The best outcome that could happen in response to the challenge of . . . is _____
2. That best outcome will happen if I _____

Try answering both those questions. It might seem impossible when you first look at them, but make an effort! You're trying to take control of your thinking in a case like this, and just because your first thoughts are full of disaster doesn't mean you can't replace those thoughts with something better. Feel free to think big. Your thoughts of disaster weren't calm, rational, and measured, so don't feel the need to be that way in counteracting them. Once you feel your positive mindset has reasserted itself, you can trim your sails a little—if you need to. But stay open to the possibility that you've actually found a way to turn a negative situation around.

Having a PMA is a blessing that you confer on yourself. No one else can ever take it away from you. If you find that you've let your PMA get weak—or you've lost it altogether—don't despair. You can decide at any moment, no matter where you are and what you're doing, to recreate it. It can fill you to bursting in an instant and put you back in control when things seem completely off course.

Of course, your PMA is far more valuable if you work at maintaining it all the time. It buoys you up, keeps you from being overwhelmed, and gives you the energy to do what needs to be done. You're going to be very pleased with PMA as it grows stronger for you, and you'll be pleasantly surprised by how it starts to influence the people around you. After all, one motivated, positive person can light up a whole room and give everybody a glow.

What do you think would happen if your PMA were to overlap with the PMA of someone else? And what if you and that person were trying to do the same things, traveling the same road?

Are you sensing the potential for something very powerful and exciting?

You better believe it.

Chapter 2

Thinking in Sync

"A person has complete control over but one thing,
and that is the power of one's thoughts."

—Napoleon Hill

THE POWER OF THOUGHT

Master Mind alliances depend on the knowledge of how
human beings think and behave. To make a Master Mind
alliance flourish, you need to be in control of your own
thoughts, which is why it's so important that you begin
developing PMA as soon as possible. If you—or anyone you
draw into your Master Mind—are dominated by negative
thinking, you're not going to get very far. In fact, you'll
probably drive each other deeper into negative territory.

The Master Mind alliance depends on the ability of one
human mind to influence and draw on the thoughts of
another mind. When Napoleon Hill first described it, he
compared the brain to a shortwave radio set, which both
broadcasts and receives messages. That was a state-of-
the art metaphor, but technology, following the model

of human thinking, has given us a closer example in the computer network: a series of independent processors linked together and sharing data, but each processor capable of working on a different task at the same time.

In a network, cables, phone lines, and infrared connections tie all those processors together and give them the ability to share information and coordinate tasks. Human beings don't have that kind of mechanical apparatus. What can connect our minds so that we can function as a Master Mind group?

Our thoughts themselves have the power to make the link.

Walk into any church on a Sunday morning, and you'll find a group of people whose minds are joined together as part of the worship service. Different congregations have different worship styles: some are quiet and reverent, while others are vibrant and full of boisterous praise. Of course, people choose their churches based on differing ideas of what they want from a service, so you can assume they've all come with some expectations of what things will be like. It's very unlikely that you'll find a pew full of people on their feet and shouting "Praise the Lord!" right in front of a pew where all have their heads bowed in silent contemplation.

A congregation has an infectious mood, and a particular spirit will dominate it. Some of the people there will have come ready to express that spirit. Others will be there because they feel a need to join into that spirit: they want to be swept up in the experience they know will be created. Most likely, the minister, or whoever is leading the service, will be working hard through readings and sermons to help shape the feeling that everyone shares. And when the service is over, if you stand outside and talk to people, they'll still be carrying the same spirit with them.

The connection that worship creates happens because a human mind is susceptible to the influences of other human minds. A church congregation is composed of people who come seeking that connection, but their experience depends on the ability of one mind to affect another. Similar connections happen when a group of people who don't know each other find themselves in an extraordinary circumstance, such as a concert by a powerful singer or a political rally featuring a gifted speaker. Certainly, there are sounds, words, and symbols influencing people there as well, but as you probably know, the mood that is created is far more than the sum of its parts. Would you want to be the only person in a concert hall listening to your favorite singer? Of course not. Part of the experience you crave is being caught up in the mood of hundreds or thousands of other people experiencing the same thrill. You want the connection.

A Master Mind operates on the same basis. But instead of making a connection between a group of people who may not know each other, it can hum along twenty-four hours a day. The members of the Master Mind can be in different rooms, different buildings—even different states—and still enjoy the rapport and energy boosts that people get in church or at a concert.

Beyond that spiritual uplift, the members of an alliance share the labor of their common task, each one of them doing the jobs for which they are best suited. They also learn from each other and inspire each other: their imaginations start to spark off each other, allowing them to think up new approaches to problem-solving. Everyone gets to share the sense of completion that comes when one person finishes a task, and anyone who's feeling blocked or frustrated knows that he or she can turn to another member for support, encouragement, and help.

This bond between members is called a *Master Mind alliance* because each participant contributes to a pool of mental energy that each one of the members can tap into. It's as if there is an extra member of the alliance who can be anywhere, at any time, to offer support, creativity, and inspiration just when it's needed most. You might even think of it as creating a guardian angel for yourself, a spirit whose only purpose is to help you achieve a worthwhile goal.

Many people who participate in a Master Mind group discover that the qualities of some of the other members begin to rub off on them. Technical details that used to seem beyond understanding become clearer. Someone's great sense of humor infects everyone else. A gift for imagination begins to manifest itself in even the most plodding thinkers. One person's ability to throw himself into a job starts showing up in other members. The whole process is exciting, not just because of the goal it can achieve but also because of the way that people share with and learn from each other.

That excitement, that sense of personal growth and discovery, isn't just a side effect of a Master Mind alliance. It's really the true purpose of forging a link with other people: to strengthen who you are and expand the possibilities of what you can do.

LINKING WITH A PURPOSE

To begin creating a Master Mind alliance, you must have a clear goal in mind. At this stage, you may not have a clear idea of what you want to accomplish in life, but don't worry about that yet. For the moment, treat this chapter as a lesson on how people think and work together toward a common goal. Don't feel you have to have a working alliance before the sun goes down tomorrow.

I gave you the example of a church service earlier because, in many ways, a Master Mind alliance works in the same fashion, as a spiritually solid congregation. It has a specific goal (spiritual welfare) that incorporates many short-term aims, such as comforting those in need, affirming a common faith, and acknowledging milestones in life (birth, marriage, and death). The members of the congregation have different contributions to make, just like the members of a Master Mind do. Some have greater financial power, some have important knowledge, and some are bedrocks of determination and enthusiasm.

The great difference between a congregation and a Master Mind alliance lies in how it comes together. Churches reach out to new members and welcome anyone willing to share in their beliefs. A Master Mind alliance is specifically assembled, usually by one person, and its members are chosen carefully and deliberately. The two most important criteria for members are (1) the ability to contribute a skill needed to do the job and (2) the ability to work in harmony with others.

Strong Master Minds are formed around people whose abilities and strengths complement each other. Sometimes, each member of the alliance comes from a very different background and has a particular specialty. But even in cases where all the members come from the same profession, close examination will show that each one has a unique quality that makes that person important to the alliance. A Master Mind of researchers at a scientific institute investigating a new theory might be composed of a brilliant theorist, a dogged experimenter, another person who is always up to date with what other scientists are doing, a fourth person with a gift for winning grant money for the team's work, and someone else who shines at finding practical applications for the results of the research.

In composing your own Master Mind group, you'll need to be frank about the qualities you need in the various members. If you need someone who can contribute money, find that person. If you need specialized knowledge, find someone who has it. Don't select people just because you like them. It's very tempting, when you're first starting out, to draw in friends and family members because they are familiar and you feel you can rely on them to be supportive. There's nothing wrong with recruiting someone close to you, but whomever you choose has to offer something you can point to and say, "We need that, and no one else can offer it."

The size of your group will depend on the purpose you've selected. You may need three people, seven people, thirteen, or more. Andrew Carnegie's Master Mind alliance consisted of approximately twenty people dedicated to the goal of efficiently producing and marketing steel.

The other criterion you must apply in selecting members of your Master Mind is whether each of the people can function well in a team. Some brilliant people simply can't get along with other people. They may be prima donnas, they may be poor communicators, or they may resent the pressure of being responsible to a group. Don't select people like this.

> Competition, laziness, and resentment will poison any chances at harmony.

In a Master Mind alliance, remember that you're trying to link all of your members together into a mental network. You want people to share the energy and excitement of your common task, and you want them to give freely to each other. You must have harmony for this to take place.

Members must be at ease and have respect for each other. Competition, laziness, and resentment will poison any chances at harmony, and soon, people will be looking out for themselves rather than for the alliance.

OFFERING REWARDS

You want to persuade a group of people to work with you and to give you things you don't have yourself. But why exactly would they do this?

To begin with, these people must share your sense of importance of the goal you're pursuing together. Whether your mutual aim is a new park in your neighborhood or a stronger, lighter alloy, you won't be able to attract anyone who doesn't agree that the aim is worthwhile and that the chances for achieving it are greater by joining your Master Mind alliance.

You'll need to offer people other motivations as well. It's human nature to seek personal improvement, and you won't attract members if you don't offer them something more than your mutual goal as a reward. They must have a motive. Exactly what you offer your members in the way of a motive will have to be carefully worked out between you both, but I'd like to shine a little light here on what Napoleon Hill called the ten basic motives:

1. Self-preservation
2. Love
3. Fear
4. Sex
5. Desire for life after death
6. Freedom, mental and physical
7. Anger
8. Hate
9. Desire for recognition and self-expression
10. Wealth

Which of these motives you employ to attract and reward people in your alliance will depend on your goals and the members you need. Each item can be a very effective motivator, but no doubt you've noted a few dark elements in the above list. In truth, any of these motives can have a dark side—people do terrible things in the name of every one. Motives such as fear, anger, and hate can inspire people to work very hard, but they also have a strong potential for infecting the harmony of your Master Mind alliance with very unpleasant qualities. While you might not choose to offer these dark motives to people, you may discover that they are acting on them anyway. You'll need to carefully consider what to do if this happens.

Fear and anger aren't necessarily bad motivators. They can be perfectly justifiable responses to a situation. If you're trying to reduce crime in your community, you'll probably find much fear and anger in the people you need to work with. But a careful leader of a Master Mind alliance will usually get better results—and have a more enjoyable experience—if he or she can redirect members toward more positive motives. If I were leading a neighborhood Master Mind group in an anti-crime effort, I'd try to appeal to people's desire for self-preservation and freedom, along with their love of family. This would make it easier to focus their attention on solutions, rather than revenge, and help give them a stronger sense of unity.

As for people motivated by hate, I stay clear of them. Hate has produced many achievements over human history, some of which have become a part of our culture and everyday lives. Much of our modern technology has its roots in things developed for warfare, for instance. There is no denying hatred's power as a motivator. But hatred requires such a complete rejection of others that it blinds people to ideas and poisons their interactions with even those they love. If someone in a Master Mind is driven by hate, that hatred will fester within the alliance and put every participant at risk.

Never overlook the importance of the desire for recognition and self-expression.

Never overlook the importance of the desire for recognition and self-expression. No matter what goal you're pursuing, you'll find that most people are hungry for these things. You might be the leader of your alliance, but that should never mean hogging all the glory for yourself. Share the limelight with those inside your group and outside of it. Recognition is often a way of persuading someone who is reluctant to be a member of your alliance to participate, particularly someone with money to contribute.

As for wealth, this is a motive that people employ all the time, especially in business-related Master Minds. Wealth is both a powerful motive and a touchy one. If someone thinks he's not getting his fair share of the money, he's going to be very unhappy, and discord will spring up with a vengeance in your alliance. The same potential is there if any reward seems to be parceled out disproportionately to others. For this reason, it's important to agree from the beginning on how rewards will be distributed. Talk freely and frankly with people about this topic. Be willing to do a little horse trading if necessary, and keep everything open and above board so that each member knows what to expect.

You may discover that some people don't care at all about some benefits and are fixated on others. As the leader of the alliance, you may be called upon to do more than your share of giving things up and making concessions. Don't resist this too much. You don't want to end up in a situation where you do all the work and get none of the benefits, but keep in mind that as the instigator of this alliance, you're probably the person with the most at stake and the most to gain from the successful achievement of its goals. You may get few or no short-term benefit in exchange for a great long-term payoff.

Remember as well that if people see you working to accommodate them, they will be willing to work harder on your behalf. Some people might take your accommodation as a sign of weakness and try to exploit it, so you better not have someone like that in your alliance. They will treat the other members in the same fashion, and soon you'll have discord on your hands.

Getting a Master Mind alliance going takes some doing. You're going to have to work hard to keep it functioning too, so let's turn our attention to the mechanics of an ongoing alliance and how you can keep things running smoothly.

KEEPING THE JUICE FLOWING

Your alliance members aren't physically connected the way a computer network is. The link between them occurs because their minds are working in harmony. Anything that disrupts this harmony has the same effect as unplugging a computer from the network. The computer no longer has the ability to draw on the resources of other machines on the network, and nothing it has is available to anyone else on the network. The network's power decreases, and all the other machines become less useful.

The first step in keeping your alliance working in a state of harmony is to have the members meet regularly, at least once a week. At these meetings, people should talk freely about what they've been doing, the problems they've been facing, and the successes they've had. This type of discussion is important because it gives people the chance to directly offer support and encouragement to each other. Each member is also kept up to date on the Master Mind's progress toward its goals and made aware of any special needs it has.

Members should feel free to talk about problems and obstacles in these meetings, and they shouldn't feel as if they're letting people down by admitting that a roadblock exists. Even if no one can offer an immediate solution, it's important that people understand that other members may be struggling with something for the moment. People gain a sense of connection and lose their sense of isolation when problems are shared. It would be much worse for someone to hide a difficulty for weeks while everyone else assumes things are going smoothly. A nasty surprise at the last minute will erode the link between alliance members and make them suspect that they can't trust each other.

Meetings should be held at regular times and in regular places. If a member of your alliance is unable to be there physically, do everything you can to bring him or her to the meeting another way. Consider participation by phone, computer instant messaging, or virtual forums such as Zoom. If that won't work, maybe a recorded report will. A voice recording is better than a written report because the sound of a voice helps make a person seem more vividly there.

Communication between members should take place outside meetings as well. Encourage people to call, text, and email each other, or just drop by each other's offices as often as possible. They don't necessarily have to have business to discuss: they just need to keep the bond between them fresh. A good word from another person in the Master Mind group may be all it takes to help a member finish a job or overcome an obstacle.

Be alert to possible sources of discord in your alliance.

If you're the leader of the alliance, you should touch base with each member frequently, sometimes every day. Sometimes the work in progress will warrant substantive discussions. Sometimes you'll just be offering a friendly word. Do your best, though, to avoid giving people the impression that you're checking up on them. No one likes to feel watched. You don't have to ask for a status report; just remind people that you're all part of the same group.

Be alert to possible sources of discord in your alliance. Act quickly to head them off. If two people have conflicting ideas about how to proceed, make sure they talk things through rather than letting each head off in their own direction. Feel perfectly free to remind them about what's at stake and what can be achieved if they work out their problems. Enlist other members of the alliance to help preserve harmony.

Sometimes, you may have to cut someone loose from your Master Mind alliance. People change, and a productive member may stop being useful to the group for all kinds of reasons. Don't present this severing as a banishment, though. Talk about why you're making this choice, and make it clear that you'd be willing to have the person back if it becomes possible for him or her to participate fully again. Those who are simply overwhelmed will be grateful to know that you haven't closed a door, and that they can very well become a valuable part of the Master Mind group again later.

MICRO MASTER MINDS

The work involved in running a Master Mind is significant. Most people find that it's too hard to participate in several large alliances at once. But the Master Mind system is very adaptable, and one of the most exciting forms it can take is a two-person alliance in which there isn't really a leader but simply two people working together very intensely. The following are examples of two-person Master Minds to give you some ideas of how you can apply the concept to your own situations.

At work. An on-the-job Master Mind alliance between you and a work colleague has many positives built in. You're physically close to each other, you share in the same company culture, and your goals and priorities usually mesh from the start. You may not even need to schedule a weekly meeting because you're in constant contact. An important issue is whether you form an alliance with someone below you on the corporate ladder, someone in a parallel position, or someone further up. Different objectives may call for different alliances.

Different objectives may call for different alliances.

Each potential alliance has different strengths. If you draw in someone whose career hasn't progressed as far as yours has, you'll inspire a lot of goodwill and win strong loyalty. Form an alliance with someone in an equal position, and you'll have a partner you won't need to educate and who you can assume needs little direction. Someone higher up the company ladder can offer you more experience and probably some powerful leverage. And it's certainly possible to have several such alliances on the job.

A Master Mind that links a couple helps erase barriers.

At home. If you're married or living with a partner, the goals of this Master Mind can be multifaceted. You can help advance each other's careers and concentrate on keeping your relationship strong and supportive for the pair of you. Even if your spouse isn't a go-getter the way you are, you'll create many good things for each other. A Master Mind that links a couple helps erase barriers that arise due to different jobs; your triumphs are your partner's triumphs and vice versa.

Pursuing your definite major purpose takes tremendous energy and dedication, and the person you live with is going to feel this almost as much as you do. A Master Mind alliance involves you both in the decisions and rewards of your dedication. It also keeps you fully aware of what's going on in your relationship, and it's much easier to address problems as soon as they arise rather than finding yourself feeling lost and confused after a casual comment turns into a heated argument, doors are slammed, and someone is sleeping on the couch.

Few of us like to succeed alone. If you have a robust Master Mind alliance with your partner, every little victory will be sweeter, and the great ones will be even more thrilling when you come home to someone who has shared in their achievement.

In education. Going after whatever it is you want most in life may very well require that you gain knowledge, and often, this requires study of some sort. It may be formal schooling at a university or occasional classes in a particular subject. Look on your instructors as people who can offer you more than class lessons and a good grade.

The best teachers thrive on encountering minds that are eager and ready to blossom. Show these traits and you'll know when you've met up with this kind of teacher. Ask for help as you need it and for suggestions for additional learning on your own. An instructor who takes an interest in your education can help guide you to fields where your skills will thrive. Learning will become exciting, rather than a chore, and it can last long past the end of the class and the term.

In your community. Everyone is enriched by some kind of community involvement, whether it's at the school, at

church, in a local theater group, or with a business or professional group. These kinds of interests keep you connected to the larger world, expose
you to new things, and keep your
mind sharp.

Find someone who has no
other connection with the rest of
your life except this outside interest, and forge a Master Mind
group. The alliance's goal doesn't have to be anything
more complicated than increasing your enjoyment of
things you do together. Whatever time you have to devote
to your mutual activity will become more exciting and rewarding for the pair of you.

> The most fascinating, exciting, and rewarding results of an alliance are the effects on you.

There are tangible benefits to any Master Mind alliance,
and those benefits come in many forms—from money to
access to goods and services. But there can be a more important aspect of a Master Mind alliance. The most fasci-
nating, exciting, and rewarding results of such an alliance
are the effects on you. There's no way you can open yourself
up to the mental communication of an alliance without
becoming a richer person in terms of energy, knowledge,
and a sense of what you're capable of accomplishing.

It's fine if your first Master Mind alliance is something
small, with a concrete goal that can be met in a month
or two. In fact, that might just be the best way to begin
because the thrill you get from reaching your goal will
be an amazing stimulus to all your subsequent efforts to
achieve your objectives. That first small alliance will lead
you on to bigger, more challenging alliances, and it will

feed your hopes and your hunger for doing something greater with your life.

What you want to achieve is entirely up to you. By now, you've probably got plenty of ideas about what that is and how you can go about it. With that excitement in mind, it's time we took a look at crystallizing your hopes into something concrete that you can begin to pursue.

Chapter 3

Understanding What You Want

"You may have everything you desire, or its equivalent, if you want it badly enough, if you are willing to pay its fair price."

—Napoleon Hill

What is important to you?

The first part of this chapter should help you find ways to express what you want in life by helping you examine all the things you think you want. Some of them may seem contradictory, but don't worry about that. You may also find that you have a huge list of what constitutes happiness, but by looking at this list, you can refine it so that a clear idea emerges. Once that happens, you'll be able to start making a plan for getting what you want.

WAIT! I KNOW WHAT I WANT!

If you feel you already have a clear idea of what you want, you're in a great position to begin getting it. But don't skip over the next section. While this section is most useful for people who are struggling to define what personal success means for them, it's also important in helping you get ready to develop a plan for success. You'll need to crystallize your ideas in order to create a plan, and the steps here will show you how to do that.

You may also discover that your idea of success is less clear than you once thought. Sometimes, we focus on aspects of success without realizing that the targets we've set are only a piece of a whole. For example, we think we want money, when in truth, money is simply a means to independence and respect.

Your current personal definition of what you want might also include things that you haven't really chosen for yourself, or the path you've set out on may have been dictated by some assumptions about yourself that are worth reexamining. It may be that something bigger is in your future—or maybe even something simpler.

Go through the exercise that follows with an open mind. The investment of time and effort is small compared to the satisfaction you'll find when you truly begin working for what you really want.

FREE FANTASY

This book frequently encourages you to focus your thinking, to winnow out distractions, and to concentrate your mind. But there are times when it's useful to cast a very wide net over your thoughts and see what you find there. Especially when you're just beginning to sort through your own ideas and understand how you think and why, you need to be free to experiment and test. You don't have to worry about latching on to the right idea immediately. Personal insight requires being open and not censoring your thoughts.

Take some time, as long as you need, to think about all the things you want in life. What would make you happy and proud of yourself? Think about money, time, family, friends, health, community, religion, education, or anything else that occurs to you.

As a picture begins to emerge in your mind, jot down some notes in your notebook. Try to be specific. Don't skip things that seem trivial now, and feel completely free to be as expressive in your notes as in your actual thoughts. If you want to own your own island, put it down. If you want a divorce, write it down. The purpose of fantasizing like this is to make yourself aware of all the elements that contribute to your idea of success.

Personal insight requires being open and not censoring your thoughts.

Keep writing as long as you need to. You'll know when you've finished because you'll feel like you're reaching for ideas, dredging up something that is so minor that you'd never want to invest the time it took to make it happen.

Now look your notes over. Ask yourself if there aren't some categories in what you've written. You may find some things that relate to money, some to time, some to relationships—you get the idea. On a fresh sheet of paper, make headings for each of these categories, and start sorting your ideas about success. You can include a miscellaneous category if you want. Leave lots of room between the categories. If there's something important that doesn't fit anywhere else, give it a category of its own.

As you start sorting your ideas this way, you'll find that many of the specific items are very similar. Draw lines between these items in your list or mark them with symbols: an asterisk, a check mark, a dot, or anything that helps you see connections.

When you've sorted everything, look at each of the categories. Spend some time thinking about whether there isn't some broad way to describe the ideas represented in each. You might write things like, "more time for family," "freedom from money worries," or "professional respect." Don't worry about including every item in one of these general statements. You don't have to be exhaustive here; you're just trying to get a feeling for things right now.

This is a detail-oriented procedure, and it can seem very mechanical. Put any feelings like that aside for the moment, though, and look at the summaries you've written. Among them will be something that stands out, something that gives you a sense of realization that seems bigger than the few words you've written, something that is positive and more important than all the others. Circle it.

Now take a moment to ask yourself if getting this thing would also bring you what you needed to take care of any of the other things you've written down. Without feeling that my examples have to be the pattern for your own answers, ponder things like whether a career change might give you financial security or the time to pay more attention to your health. Maybe you'll find that something in your life is standing as an obstacle to enjoying those other things. It could be a problem with self-esteem or a dependency on alcohol or drugs.

You don't have to decide at this moment that whatever you've circled is your major purpose. And your major purpose isn't something that has to determine who you are and what you do for the rest of your life. For many people, achieving a major goal only awakens them to other things they can do and become. Don't feel that somehow this thing you've circled places a limit on you.

Take a while or so to think about the idea you've circled. Is it exciting? Does it suggest completeness to you? Do you really want it?

For the moment, don't worry about how possible it seems. If it implies big changes in your life, you can make them. If it requires money you don't have right now, you can get it. You can achieve anything you believe in. Just ask yourself whether you want to believe in it.

The opinions of colleagues and family members can be very important, but they can also be confining or diverting.

Some people find that the first thing they circle doesn't truly awaken a lasting sense of realization or excitement for them. There are several explanations for this. Sometimes, you can be so weighed down by ideas that other people have about who you are and what you can do that you end up circling something based on other people's ideas. The opinions of colleagues and family members can be very important, but they can also be confining or diverting.

If you suspect that somehow you've let yourself be limited or misled this way, repeat the exercise above. This time, don't hold anything back. Make sure you're completely free with yourself when it comes to your hopes. Even if what you wind up with is surprising, spend the next day letting yourself imagine what it would be like to achieve it.

For some people, the idea they circled is still somehow a shadow of what they really want. The definition of success they circled focused on an aspect of something much larger. For example, the idea of owning your own business may be part of a desire for independence; completing a novel or a play may merely be a means of the larger goal of expressing a creative impulse. If you think this applies to you, repeat the exercise, but focus it on the idea that was a near miss for you. It may be that you were closer than you ever realized to knowing what you want out of life.

THE BALANCING ACT

Many people are surprised when they realize what they want most out of life. Sometimes, they resist the idea intellectually because it conflicts with other ideas they have about who they are and what they actually do in life.

A classic example is the struggle, for both men and women, between family and career priorities. Owning your own successful business just doesn't seem to leave as much time for children and romance. Devoting as much energy to your loved ones as you want seems to make charging up the corporate ladder impossible.

But there are other tensions as well. The work you want to be doing may seem wildly at odds with your current situation in life. If you're working in a department store, it may seem impossible to you that you can go to law school.

If you've spent years to become successful in your job, it may seem like you're throwing that all away to found your own start-up company, to open a bed and breakfast, or to devote yourself to breeding championship dachshunds.

> **It's important to remember that whatever you want most in life isn't the only thing you want in life.**

It's important to remember that whatever you want most in life isn't the only thing you want in life. Admit this to yourself, and it will be easier to recognize what your greatest priority is. You don't have to thrust everything else aside to achieve it.

CAREER

A career is the time-honored way to mark yourself as a successful person. Usually, that involves rising to an important and lucrative position, as well as enjoying professional recognition and the esteem of other people in the same field.

But a common trap for young people is the assumption that up-up-up is the only way to go. If you are district manager this year, you should be shooting for regional manager. Just made associate vice president? Then you must be aiming for a full VP position, adding "executive" to your title soon after that. That's one path, and, for many people, it's the right one.

But it's worth considering if it's the wrong one for you.

There's a famous idea, called the Peter Principle, that says people are promoted within an organization until they reach one level above what they are truly capable of doing. While they handled all their previous jobs well, eventually they get a new position that they can't fill as effectively, and that's where their promotions end. It's a little depressing when you consider the implications.

> Don't limit your ambitions, but give careful thought to whether you're seeking advancement for its own sake.

A bigger office isn't always better. Think about the things you enjoy about your work, and ask yourself whether those same factors would remain promotion after promotion. Executive positions often involve a very different set of responsibilities, and you might not want them all.

Don't limit your ambitions, but give careful thought to whether you're seeking advancement for its own sake or for the status or money it confers, instead of for the way it will affect what you do at your job. You might not be the first person who finds that administration and meetings take you away from rolling up your sleeves to do the things that first interested you about your career.

Now let's consider the romantic relationship of your life, if there is one currently. Every relationship is founded on some assumptions about the roles the people in it may play. Those roles may be traditional or highly unconventional, but both of you have been making choices based on those assumptions.

You may need to fundamentally alter some of those assumptions to pursue your major purpose. If so, you'll need to talk about it, engage in some honest negotiations, and be keenly alert to the implications of those changes. And even then, you'll need to prepare yourself for some surprises. One or both of you may feel that the new arrangements are unsatisfying or unfair. Or, you may find them energizing and exciting. Pursuing your goal isn't an automatic threat to your love life or marriage. Indeed, a happier, more satisfied you can revitalize the relationship, help it survive rocky times, and take it to new levels.

But you do need to talk openly and honestly about the changes you foresee. You need to remain open to adaptation as things go along, even occasionally deferring something you want. You need not become the secondary figure, but just be willing to offer the same give-and-take that you're asking for.

Unfortunately, there are some who find that their plans are in complete conflict with the basis of their relationships. This presents some painful, wrenching choices. You may be able to find a way around these conflicts, but if that path involves secrets and denials, or a significant impediment to attaining your major purpose, then you may need to move on.

If you're involved with someone whose understanding of what you want and need in life is so radically different from what you understand, then other problems will arise very soon. If your plans are completely under someone else's thumb, you'll be miserable. You'll make other people miserable, starting with the person you love.

I urge you to talk about this with your partner to make your feelings as clear as possible before you take any action. Maybe the depth of your feelings will be persuasive or will at least open a discussion that seemed closed. But you may simply have to leave.

If you're not in a relationship now, things will probably be simpler. It's entirely possible that romance and children simply aren't big factors in what you want and won't be an issue. But if they are, and things begin to get serious with someone, it's obvious that you need to be clear about where you're going in life and what you want to do. Some couples find that their goals mesh incredibly well. But even for those with different ambitions, it's very possible that your relationship can thrive and work for you both, as long as you understand where your goals overlap.

It's impossible to approach romance in a mechanical fashion as unpredictability is one of its most exciting and enjoyable rewards. But thoughtfulness and clarity about what you want in a relationship will help you make sure that you get what you need while offering your loved ones the same thing.

Now let's think about money. Everyone, it's been said, has a price. Do you know yours?

Usually, that comment is made with cynical implications, but it's essential to understand how you think about money and why you regard it as important (or unimportant).

Money is such a fluid thing. Its convertibility into objects or services is a great part of why we value it. But it has an allure of its own. Being able to say you have a million dollars in the bank (or in the stock market) has a ring of security and status about it.

Is that what you want it for?

Much of the time, money is a stand-in for something else: freedom, power, prestige. There may be nothing wrong with any of these things, but if you mistake money for the thing it represents, you may make sacrifices that take you away from what you really regard as part of your success.

The most obvious example is someone who works and works and works with an eye on nothing more than net worth. Family, recreation, creativity, and independence all take a back seat to the accumulation of dollars. People may stay in a high-paying job they hate because they can't imagine giving up the money.

> **Much of the time, money is a stand-in for something else: freedom, power, prestige.**

If money represents a significant part of your ambitions, spend a lot of time clarifying what it's for, and when and how you'll take advantage of that money. If you want to retire at a certain age and travel, make sure that retirement and traveling are the goals you focus on, not cash. If you want a house in a certain place, a particular car, and a lifestyle you've thought of for years, keep those goals in your sights.

Money alone as a goal is probably the easiest thing to achieve. If it's all that matters to you, you can make all kinds of changes in your life to get it. You can cut your living expenses to the bone, stop socializing, take a second job, not worry about clothes or recreation, and go without small luxuries.

Not that appealing, is it?

So, examine your ideas about money closely and try to connect them to other ambitions. Understand what you want money for, before you commit yourself to anything. And, as with any other thing you want, remain willing to examine what you're giving up to secure it and what you're getting in return.

ASSEMBLING THE PIECES

Assuming that you've taken some time to get to know your ideas about success, you can now begin shaping them into something definable. This is another process full of give-and-take, with nothing written in stone while you work at it. The only person you're accountable to right now is yourself.

> Understand what you want money for, before you commit yourself to anything.

Ideally, you want to develop a short written statement of what you want out of life. A single sentence is best—as clear and as specific as you can make it. This sentence should also be wholehearted, encompassing the fullest, most positive description of your major purpose. You want to be motivated when you read it. This is your statement of purpose—your mission statement.

Writing something like this may come easy to you, or you may find it hard to do. If you struggle, don't give up or settle for something that just seems close. The more precise and certain you are in your writing, the more likely you are to get what you want. You're always free to make changes in this statement, but if your goals are big, write them that way.

Your statement of purpose is something you'll be referring to often as you work. If you hold something back—a goal that you don't dare include now, for example—you won't really be aiming yourself at that wish.

Writing this statement can be very intimidating and overwhelming. In part, you'll be writing out a definition of how far you are from the thing that will make you happiest. And, for some people, the very idea that a single sentence can describe all the things they want from life seems absurd. But you aren't limiting yourself in any way by what you write, and you aren't admitting to being a bad person by saying you want to become a better one. You're writing your statement of purpose solely for your own use and benefit.

> **The more precise and certain you are in your writing, the more likely you are to get what you want.**

Here are some examples of how you might write such a statement of purpose. They're entirely hypothetical, and they are here only to inspire you and show you it's okay to be very concrete as long as what you write is truly what matters to you:

- I will become a doctor by my fiftieth birthday.
- I will succeed Wilson as CEO.
- I will have $2,000,000 in savings at retirement.
- I will give my family a happy and wonderful home where they know they are loved and safe.
- I will publish my poetry.

- I will be elected to City Council in the next election.
- I will become the most respected lawyer in town.
- I will become a professional actor.
- I will publish my own investment newsletter and make a profit of $200,000 a year at it.

These are only examples, of course, and if your own statement isn't anything like them, then congratulations! You don't need to fit into anyone else's ideas about success. You only need to satisfy yourself.

If you wish, you can add a sentence or two more, specifying the conditions in other areas that need to be met for you to feel truly successful. This is useful if

You don't need to fit into anyone else's ideas about success.

you feel you're going to have to work hard to reconcile your purpose with other responsibilities. It's also a good way to remind yourself that your purpose is part of a vision of your entire life. Having $10 million won't satisfy you if you're also the most hated person in town.

Make a small copy of your statement of purpose that you can keep with you always. I mean *always*. It should fit in your wallet or go in your pocket if you always have one. You'll want and need to pull it out and refer to it at different times. Sometimes, you'll just need it to stiffen your backbone when making a choice. Sometimes, you'll need a boost when facing disappointment or tackling something difficult.

You should also make a ritual of reading your statement of purpose three times a day. Read it once soon after you get out of bed, a second time in the middle of the day, and again before you go to sleep. I suggest reading it three times in succession as well, just for emphasis. Whenever you can, read it aloud. Hearing yourself speaking the words only adds to the reinforcement you're giving yourself. Reading your statement of purpose is precisely about reinforcing your determination to succeed. It reminds you of what you want, why you're doing what you're doing throughout the day, and what kind of satisfaction you're going to have when you accomplish it.

> **Reading your statement of purpose is precisely about reinforcing your determination to succeed.**

YOU PROBABLY FIGURED THIS OUT, BUT . . .

These steps based on Napoleon Hill's ideas won't work if your major purpose involves hurting other people. Revenge and deceit are motivations that this success system cannot incorporate. Negative experiences motivate people all the time. Some of the richest people on the planet have risen from abject poverty. Civil rights leaders and medical researchers are motivated by a desire to overcome flaws in the world. A campaign for the school board can begin in dissatisfaction with the local educational system. These are all responses

> **Revenge and deceit are motivations that this success system cannot incorporate.**

to negative situations, but they are expressed in positive actions.

Your major purpose may have been formed, in part, by bad things that have happened to you. You may want to put them behind you, or help other people avoid similar experiences. This is good and no-ble. But if you express what you want in terms of getting back at whoever caused you hurt, you'll be building your plans on a profoundly hollow and un-stable foundation. Your response to whatever happened to you should be one that enriches your own life at no one else's expense, no matter how terribly they may have treated you.

Let's make sure that what you do pays off.

By now, you've put your finger on what you want in life. By describing it, you make it concrete, attainable, and real. You're connected at last to something very valuable to yourself.

And you're probably very eager to start doing something about it.

Let's make sure that what you do pays off.

Chapter 4

Making Your Plan

"If you have no major purpose, you are drifting toward certain failure."

—Napoleon Hill

If you're familiar with Napoleon Hill's writing, you'll recognize that this chapter is about something that isn't usually dealt with on its own. But creating a map of your path to success is a step that trips up many people. They have a clear idea of what they want; they know how to start thinking positively; but they just can't envision all the milestones they have to pass to achieve what they want.

You won't get what you want out of life without a plan.

You may not care if the world ever notices what you achieve, or you may plan to leave your mark on politics, medicine, physics, or the arts for generations to come. But it doesn't matter because you won't get what you want out of life without a plan.

Of course, your plan may alter as your ambitions change or as new opportunities arise. Your plan is your tool for achieving your major purpose. You're going to become a guided missile locked onto a target that exists. You're going to become someone who is making daily progress toward what you want—progress that you can measure, take satisfaction from, and celebrate.

CREATING THE FRAMEWORK

Having read this far, you've already arrived at a positive expression of your own idea of success. While you were developing this statement, your mind was probably suggesting all kinds of reasons why you could *not* achieve your major purpose. That's fine, because now you're going to use those negative ideas for a positive purpose. You're going **Any negative ideas you had are simply things you'll overcome as you advance toward your goal.** to incorporate them into your plan for getting what you want. In that plan, any negative ideas you had are simply things you'll overcome as you advance toward your goal.

Your own plan won't look like anyone else's, so there's no set formula for what it should look like: it can be a fifteen-step list or a paragraph that tells a story. However, your plan should have three important characteristics:

1. It should be highly specific, including dates, figures, titles, people, jobs, or any other element that you recognize as important.
2. It should address all the major things you want to accomplish.
3. It should be expressed in the most positive language at your command.

HALLMARKS OF A GOOD PLAN

Here's a list of things that appear in a strong plan. You may not need to incorporate every one of them, but running your eye down the list might help you catch a step you've left out or remind you to be specific about something you're still dealing with in a vague way.

1. Dates. *You can choose actual days (May 1) or express a chronological progression (six months), but attach a realistic, optimistic date to every significant event you possibly can. Creating a timeline can expose some weak assumptions or challenge you to realize just how quickly you can make some changes.*

2. Time allocation. *Where appropriate, try to include hours spent daily on a particular task. Consider where this time will come from. Will you have to give something up in order to create the time you need? Will you need to gain someone else's cooperation to put your plan into action?*

3. Waiting time. *Applications for classes or licenses have deadlines. Work that someone else will do for you, such as a remodeling job in your office, also has a schedule. Investigate these things so you can anticipate them. Then, you'll be better able to use your waiting time productively.*

4. People. *Name names as often as you can. If your spouse or kids are going to have to handle some of the household chores, don't be afraid to write it down. If you need to demonstrate your skills to a boss or client, include their names too. There is power in being specific.*

The following are two hypothetical plans for different people with very different goals. You'll see what's great about their plans and where they can use improvement. Your plan doesn't have to look like either of these, but they should help you see how all the important characteristics of a plan are incorporated.

LISA'S PLAN

Lisa is thirty-four and the office manager for a law firm. She started out as a secretary just out of high school, so she has plenty of experience even without much formal education. Lisa's goal is to own her own temporary agency, supplying top-notch office workers to firms in her city. She wants her agency to be the first place any business calls when they need a temporary worker. After doing some careful thinking, this is what Lisa has devised for a plan:

Goal: To be the leading temp agency in town by December 31, 20XX (a year and a half away).

1. *Complete small business start-up course at community college by December of this year.*
2. *Investigate and obtain all business licenses by December of this year.*
3. *Give two months' notice to current employer on November 1.*
4. *Rent office space for occupancy on January 2.*
5. *Recruit ten high-quality temps by business opening January 15.*

6. *Call ten different firms I know every business day be-tween January 2 and January 13 to promote the agency. Stress my reputation at the law firm and the quality of our temps.*
7. *Recruit and hire another ten temps by March 15.*
8. *Call five new firms each day once the agency is open.*
9. *Add ten more specialized temps (bookkeeping, medical office, paralegal) by June 1.*
10. *Start free training programs for temps, on the use of new office software by September 15.*
11. *Have fifty temps available for assignment by December 1.*

Lisa's plan is ambitious and generally very concrete. While the plan doesn't overflow with positive language, it's assertively and confidently written. However, there are a few things she has overlooked.

First, Lisa is going to need money to rent office space, as well as have phones installed, buy or rent office equipment, pay for office supplies, get business insurance, and so on. She is also going to have to live on something until the fees she charges begin adding up to something substantial. Her plan should address where this money will come from, as well as how much of a profit will be satisfactory.

Most likely, these things are all in the back of Lisa's head. She has an idea of how much money will be coming in from the number of temps she has working for her, but as in any business start-up, she needs to make sure that a cash crunch isn't going to snarl her plans.

In addition, Lisa wants to train her temps, which could give her a great advantage in the market, but who is going to do this? When and where will it be done? How will she identify what her temps need to learn? How long will it take to train them?

And, will Lisa be the only one in her office? Will she hire an assistant so that she can, for instance, take a lunch or a day off for an emergency? What use is the best temp agency in town if it shuts down while Lisa leaves town for a funeral?

None of these things are insurmountable problems for Lisa, of course, but if she thinks about them now and makes plans to deal with them, they won't come as surprises when she's out there working hard to make her plan happen.

Blake's Plan

Blake is a commission sales representative for a wine distributor. He sells a variety of wines imported from Spain. Spanish wines don't have a blockbuster reputation in his territory: most of his stores tell him that their customers don't know much about them and are usually interested in wines that are either inexpensive or have a prestigious reputation, such as French or Italian wines.

Blake wants to double his income in the next two years. That means at least doubling his sales volume. Here's how he's planned to go about it.

Next month, I will pick three high-volume stores, not located near each other, where I don't do much business. I will offer them a free case of a particular wine, chosen for wide appeal, and I will give up my commission on sales of that wine for a month so I can reduce the price for the store.

I will offer to spend four hours at each store on a Friday after-noon and evening, giving their customers free tastes of the wine, along with samples of Spanish food. I will do this to raise the cus-tomers' opinions of Spanish wines so that on subsequent visits, they will be more interested in buying them.

The following month, I will offer to do the same thing for three more stores. After I have done this in twelve stores, I will offer to go back to any of the stores again. I will do a tasting in at least two stores every month for the next two years.

I will invite the food editor and travel writer of the local pa-per to a tasting of Spanish wines, including wines that I do not sell, and present a traditional Spanish meal for them. I will also provide them with promotional materials from the Spanish travel bureau. I will do this in hopes of inspiring features in the paper about Spanish wine and food, or simply about Spain.

In twenty-four months, I will have doubled my sales.

Blake also has a good beginning for his plan, but he could use some refinements. To begin, he sets no incre-mental sales goals: he'd be better off deciding what sort of increases he'd like to see after six, twelve, and eighteen months. This would give him something to shoot for in the shorter term and provide benchmarks to gauge his progress. This could help him realize that he needs to be including more stores in his promotional campaign, or it might inspire him to raise his sights.

He could also be more forceful in his language. Instead of saying, "I will offer to spend four hours at each store on a Friday afternoon and evening," he could write, "I will convince each store to give me four hours on a Friday af-ternoon and evening." This states things more positively, and it emphasizes exactly what Blake will need to accomplish for his plan to go forward. If he finds himself struggling to meet his goals, Blake will have a clearer picture of what he needs to focus his attention on.

Blake should also consider drawing his company into his plans more. They'd have some resources he could use. He might not have to bear all the costs of his ideas himself. If he were in a friendly competition with a rep whose territory was near his, he could share success stories, pick up some more ideas, and accomplish more in terms of generating some enthusiasm about his products.

Neither Blake nor Lisa is incorporating a Master Mind alliance either. Lisa could be drawing in one or two of her temps, someone else with experience running her own business who might also be a good client for her agency, or perhaps someone with some cash who'll be interested in sharing profits. Blake could turn to that sales rep in the next territory, someone with the Spanish trade commission, his supervisor, or even the owner of one of the stores he sells to. They all have something to gain and could be eager to work closely with him.

Your goal and your plan may be nothing like Blake's or Lisa's, but, like theirs, it should be thorough, specific, and positive.

Feel free to mull your plan over for a week or two after you've written it down. This may help you find some holes in it, or come up with a more efficient way of accomplishing things. But two weeks is all you get. After those two weeks, and preferably sooner, you must commit yourself because it's time to begin the process of getting what you want.

ROLLING UP YOUR SLEEVES

Exactly what your first step is, only you know. The hardest part may be taking your very first step. It's natural to feel some trepidation at this point. You're about to begin making big changes in your life, and change is scary, along with being difficult. It means doing things you've never done, taking responsibility that you haven't shouldered before, and living with the consequences.

> The hardest part may be taking your very first step.

Still, you—by now a master of a PMA—need to be emphasizing the other feeling that comes with change: excitement.

I hope that in the time since you created your statement of purpose, you've been reading it at least three times each day. There is absolutely no substitute for this kind of reinforcement. Your mind, to paraphrase what Napoleon Hill said, is your most priceless asset. You should be putting it to work for you every opportunity you get. Reading your statement of purpose thrice daily is the simplest, most powerful way of deploying your number one advantage.

> Reading your statement of purpose thrice daily is the simplest, most powerful way of deploying your number one advantage.

You'll discover that the more positively written your statement is, and the more concretely you've expressed your plan, the more you'll be creating excitement. Now is

the time to begin using that excitement you've been stor-
ing up.

Many people work out their statement of purpose in private; they create their plans for success that way too, even
if they seek advice from others about specific steps. If this
is how you've worked, it's time to
share your purpose and at least
the broad outlines of your plan
with someone else. Of course,
if you're going to incorporate a
Master Mind alliance, this sharing
may be the first step in your plan.
(And if you aren't using a Master
Mind, why not? Don't throw away
that advantage!)

> Taking
> responsibility for
> your future also
> means taking
> responsibility for
> your past and
> your present, with
> all their flaws.

Sharing their purpose and plan is often what scares
people who are just beginning to set out. Once someone else knows what you're doing, you can't hide any
setbacks. You can't deny that you want to change your
life. You can't pretend that you're satisfied with the status
quo. You're admitting that your life isn't exactly what you
want it to be.

Taking responsibility for your future also means taking responsibility for your past and your present, with all
their flaws. In this way, sharing is making yourself vulnerable. You're vulnerable to criticism, vulnerable to disappointment, vulnerable to someone else's doubts.

But sharing also opens you up to a whole list of things
that are worth every bit of the vulnerability you feel. First
off, you'll gain a cheerleader or two, and those count for a

heck of a lot. You'll be able to pick up the phone and say "I did it," and hear an enthusiastic response. That reinforces your determination incredibly. You'll also be able to draw on others for help, either as a part of your plan or on the spur of the moment when you need an extra push in tackling something.

Just as important, you'll have taken a plan and given it a life of its own by sharing it. It's so easy to sit back and think, "tomorrow I'll start," when no one but you knows that you held back today and the day before. Once you've shared your plan with someone else, you've not only gone public but also admitted it to yourself in a new way. Speaking the words to another person validates them for your own mind. It's like saying "I love you" for the first time. The admission is a confirmation both to your loved one and to yourself.

> **Speaking the words to another person validates them for your own mind.**

If your plans seem so alien to your life right now that you can't imagine sharing them, please find at least some part of them that you can share. Tell someone you're taking a class, or looking for a particular promotion. Identify something that you can safely tell someone else, and tell them. You'll find that sharing a part makes it much easier to share the whole: you may feel so good about it that you reveal the whole plan.

> **Start where you stand!**

But please, do as Napoleon Hill often advised: start where you stand!

GETTING CRITICIZED

Occasionally, people share their plans with someone who can't handle the information. Instead of encouragement, they get negativity that can be hostile or just subtly dismissive. Frequently, this person is a member of their own family.

If this happens to you—and it happens on a rare occasion—you'll need to be strong. Don't dwell on the bad reaction. Consider that the person you told may be as overwhelmed by the news as you were when you began contemplating what you wanted to do and all that it meant. Someone who hasn't been working on a PMA, and hasn't devoted all the careful thought that you've put into discovering your definite major purpose and making a plan for it, may simply not be ready to accept that it's possible.

Don't devote any energy to trying to win someone over to your side at this point. If your news is a shock or a threat, you'll only get your confidant's hackles up and inspire further discussions on why you're making a mistake. Thank that person for caring about you, even if that emotion isn't at the top of the list of what you're feeling. Then end the conversation as quickly and politely as you can.

Afterward, alone if possible, spend some time reading your statement of purpose over and over. Focus your mind on what you want and what you're going to do. Don't dwell on any of the reactions you've received. Instead, bend your will to finding someone else with whom you can share your plans.

Most people discover that sharing makes it much easier to take the next, or even first, step in their plan. Their confession, if you will, of what they want is liberating and inspiring in ways they never imagined. It's an important step toward discovering a community of people who believe in you—and to realizing that you are the most important person in that community.

> **Sharing makes it much easier to take the next, or even first, step in their plan.**

HITTING SOME SPEED BUMPS

Progress toward what you want shows you parts of the landscape that you only imagined before. The new view is always exhilarating, but it can also show some curves in the road that you didn't know were there.

This is another reason you should have a Master Mind alliance established as soon as you reasonably can. You'll have other people to help you navigate new terrain or look over your shoulder for you. You'll have resources, imagination, and knowledge to draw on, which extend far beyond your own.

> **Progress toward what you want shows you parts of the landscape that you only imagined before.**

But what if you discover after implementing your plan that it isn't working? The course you plotted won't take you where you wanted to go. What then?

You adapt. Carefully, thoughtfully, and as quickly as you can.

What you don't do is take this surprise as a sign that you are a failure. There isn't a single person in all of human history who hasn't had to change course, double back, bide some time, or even eat a little crow before succeeding at what they set out to do in life. And every one of them was smarter, stronger, and ultimately more successful because of it.

Children don't stop trying to walk the first time they fall. The smallest child and the most successful people all know that there will be disappointments. But the goals they're pursuing are worth some knocks. And none of them gets up and does exactly what they did before. They alter something.

When you encounter your first setback, think first about how much you want your objective. And then start looking around for places to make changes in your plan. You may need more studying, more capital, or more associates. The needed change will be something within your grasp, that is, something you can do or get if you focus on your major purpose and your belief that you can attain it.

Don't give up. Look for alternatives. Ask other people for their insights. You may indeed have to pause for a while, but if you spend that time saying, "I'm finding another way to get what I want," you'll be much better off than complaining, "I'm stalled. I'm not getting anywhere."

If you encounter a setback, go back and read Chapter 1 on PMA. A PMA is essential to overcoming an apparent roadblock.

Whatever you do, don't give up!

CHARGE!

At this point, you may be so fired up about your plan for achieving your goal that you want to put this book down and get to work. You feel like your fate is under your control. It's like getting your driver's license. You want to get out there and burn up the road, feel the freedom, go someplace, anyplace, because now it's finally possible.

But there are twelve more chapters in this book, and every one of those chapters will help you build new skills that will only make it easier for you to get what you want most in life. You can begin right away to put your plan into effect, but first take the time to study the remaining chapters and to absorb and apply what they show you.

Each chapter that follows will show you a new way to take control of your mind, that priceless, irreplaceable asset. You'll be excited about what you learn, and you'll only grow more confident about your ability to succeed. You owe it to yourself and your major purpose to complete this book on how to fully realize your own potential.

So come along and learn what else Napoleon Hill's ideas can show you about what you can do to live life on your own terms.

Chapter 5

Starting the Fire

"A man with a definite major purpose never needs an alarm clock."

—Napoleon Hill

The change has begun. What started as a glimmer of an idea has grown into a firm belief that you can have what you want most in life. As you've given a name to what you want and created a plan for making it happen, you've become confident that it's possible. Your goal is within your grasp!

You feel energized, alive, and excited about what you can do. Old fears are fading away, and new ideas are leaping into your mind all the time. You may not know where all this energy comes from, but it's exciting, isn't it?

Yes, it's a wonderful, life-affirming sensation that sweeps over you when you think about how your life is changing and will keep on changing. And that energy, that feeling of strength and possibility, springs from inside you. No one else is creating it. You don't need anyone else's approval to feel it. You can summon it just by focusing your mind on your major purpose.

That incredible rush of confidence and power is your enthusiasm. It's a reflection of your sincere belief in yourself, increased by your desire to create a life that you live on your own terms. It's an astounding personal power that we all possess, and one of the most terrific benefits of Napoleon Hill's ideas is that they can show you how to use your enthusiasm for a purpose. Your purpose.

THE CONTROLLED BURN

Everybody has enthusiasm once in a while. Maybe you feel it when your child's soccer team takes the lead in a game. Or it might well up in you at work when you finally feel that the end of a project is in sight. You can experience enthusiasm listening to a sermon or a political speech, or when you, at last, get to take a vacation someplace you've always dreamed of going.

> That incredible rush of confidence and power is your enthusiasm.

Enthusiasm like that is an honest reaction to an exciting development. Often, it isn't created by something you've done but by the actions of someone you love or admire, someone whose success or ideas you feel a kinship to.

But most of the time, that kind of enthusiasm fades when circumstances change. Your child's team wins the game, you celebrate, and then you've got a report to write. Your vacation ends, and you're back in the familiar daily grind. The memories are great, but that rush of excitement is gone.

It doesn't have to be that way—not when it comes to the enthusiasm you feel for your major purpose. You can

When your enthusiasm takes on a life of its own, it can be disastrous.

create enthusiasm at will, strengthen it when necessary, and use it to push yourself to tackle difficult jobs, make hard decisions, build self-confidence, and enlist other people in your cause. Enthusiasm can be a powerful tool when you consciously choose to use it to achieve your goals.

But like any fire, enthusiasm needs careful monitoring. You have to be very aware of its ability to influence other people as well as yourself. When you direct your enthusiasm toward worthwhile endeavors and use it with full awareness of its effects, it is beneficial. When your enthusiasm takes on a life of its own, it can be disastrous.

A WOMAN WHO UNDERSTOOD ENTHUSIASM

Napoleon Hill loved to tell a story about himself and how he first began to understand how enthusiasm needed to be guided toward a purpose.

Hill's mother died when he was a young boy. For several years, Hill's father felt powerless as young Nap grew into the terror of the neighborhood. He was always playing pranks, disobeying his father, and getting into the messiest, most destructive types of trouble. He packed a pistol and announced to everyone that Jesse James was his idol. Few doubted it.

Eventually, Hill's father remarried. Martha Ramey Hill was a former schoolteacher who didn't blanch when her new husband introduced his son as "the worst boy in the county."

"You are wrong," she told a stunned father and son. "This is not the worst boy, but the smartest who has not yet found a proper outlet for his enthusiasm."

It was Martha who suggested that Nap's "adventures" reflected an imagination and strong drive, not a criminal bent. It was Martha who bought him a typewriter and traded it to Nap for his pistol. It was Martha who encouraged him to write his adventures and ideas down.

So, it was Martha Ramey Hill, with her understanding of enthusiasm, who set Napoleon Hill on his path to discovering the principles that you're now learning to apply in your own life.

Imagine going to buy a cell phone. In the first store you visit, you meet salesman Cliff. Cliff is so certain that you need a cell phone that he's already decided which one you need. The Sparky 800 has lots of features. It comes with a calling plan that gives you free international calling, and, best of all, it's always traceable. Anyone who tries to call you will get a message telling them where you are!

Every time you ask Cliff a question about a different phone, he waves his hand and tells you it's a piece of junk. A busy important person like you needs to be connected all the time. You need dependability, you need access—you need the Sparky 800!

Meanwhile, you're imagining what it would be like to simply grab your phone and not have to study a manual before using it. You want to be able to reach the office or the towing service in an emergency, not check the price of pork bellies in Frankfurt. And as for everyone knowing where you are, every moment of the day, that just seems like an invitation to nosy coworkers to waste more of your time asking why you were at the dentist yesterday afternoon.

You get away from Cliff as fast as you can.

Summoning the courage to try again, you go into another store. Miranda begins by asking you questions about what you want a cell phone to do for you. She's confident but respectful, and when she explains why a particular phone isn't best for your expressed needs, she never trashes any of the products she's responsible for selling. She presents you with several options and makes a recommendation that is in accord with what you want, and you leave her store with a phone that does just what you want it to do.

Both Cliff and Miranda have enthusiasm for their jobs. But Cliff's enthusiasm is out of control. He's so convinced about the benefits of the Sparky 800 that he can't imagine why anyone would want anything else. Miranda's enthusiasm, on the other hand, is targeted. Her enthusiasm is directed toward understanding what you need. It makes her knowledgeable and interested in you, and it doesn't overwhelm you. Where Cliff drives you away, Miranda leaves you feeling like you could return to her store and get good advice about another piece of equipment.

That's the difference between uncontrolled enthusiasm and enthusiasm that is properly directed. They are equally powerful, but one is just as likely to cause you difficulties as to help you. The other focuses your attention and your skills on the task at hand, makes you more aware, is more convincing, and is a pleasure to be around. It's the difference between a fire that's licking up the drapes and a warm, toasty blaze on the hearth.

FIRE MANAGEMENT

So just how do you make sure that you have the right kind of enthusiasm?

First, you need a strong PMA.

PMA is proportional.

A PMA is necessary for enthusiasm in the first place. You need to believe that what you're doing is worthwhile and possible. But keep in mind, "PMA provides the correct response to varied situations, obstacles and opportunities." In other words, PMA is proportional.

Adjust your display of enthusiasm to each person you deal with. Be like saleswoman Miranda: ask questions, evaluate what a person wants, and determine what kind of information they need to hear. Of course, you must be honest and forthright in all this, but by focusing your speech and actions on what is required, you're dis-

PMA provides the correct response to varied situations, obstacles and opportunities.

playing respect and intelligence. Those qualities make a mild show of enthusiasm much more convincing than an over-the-top display that suggests you're a little unbalanced.

Controlled enthusiasm also requires a clear knowledge of your plan for success. When you know how you're going to achieve your major purpose, you can keep your enthusiasm from sidetracking you. When a new opportunity presents itself, you can evaluate that option in terms of how it fits your plan. When you're just beginning to pursue success, you may become overenthusiastic. You can sense how much is possible for you now, and you may be tempted to grab for all of it.

This is a bad thing because it's much too easy to fill your agenda with more goals than you can ever accomplish. You'll find yourself overcommitted to conflicting obligations while running out of time, money, and steam. You'll lose the goodwill of the people who are working with you, and you'll soon find yourself farther away from what you really wanted in the first place.

With your statement of purpose and your plan a part of your daily thoughts, you'll be able to evaluate how a particular choice affects them. It's much easier to decide whether to pursue a risky reward when you know whether the reward is really important to what you want. It may not even be a reward. For example, do you need national publicity right now, before you have your staff trained in the proper way to handle new customers?

This isn't to say that controlling your enthusiasm should prevent you from seizing opportunities. Maybe you can shift resources to increase staff training before the publicity hits. You could profit tremendously from national exposure—if you think things through and prepare for it. Controlled enthusiasm doesn't always say

"No." It's much more likely to say, "Yes—if I do it the right way."

Your plan and your enthusiasm affect each other, so each must take the other into account. Often that means careful deliberation, which unbridled enthusiasm can easily prevent. But if you're clearly aware of your goals and how you want to reach them, you can make your enthusiasm do its job properly and powerfully.

Temper your awareness with honesty and a sense of proportion.

Awareness—that's what it comes down to. You need to be aware of what other people want from you, what you want from them, and what your circumstances require. Temper your awareness with honesty and a sense of proportion. Season it with a dose of passion and conviction. Then observe the effect of your enthusiasm on yourself and others.

FEEDING THE FIRE

Your enthusiasm for your major purpose is something you create. Even when it seems to well up inside of you unbidden, you've created it from your desire for what you want and your knowledge that you can have it. You are the source.

Accordingly, you can also summon enthusiasm when you need it. You can use it to convince someone, to give yourself the energy you need when you're beginning to feel exhausted, or when a flicker of doubt enters your mind. Often, all you need to do is remember your goal, and your enthusiasm will flow.

But it helps to be able to stoke the fire. Enthusiasm is the result of mental processes, and you know by now that you can control all your mental processes as you need to. You can create and reinforce the enthusiasm you need.

Some people have difficulty accepting this. They feel that enthusiasm must come from the heart. It's either there or isn't. Anything else is just fooling yourself. This is partially true, but overlooks a few points.

First, your enthusiasm for your major purpose is always there. When you're stuck on the highway with a flat tire in a driving rainstorm, soaked to your skin as you wrestle with the spare, your enthusiasm may seem the farthest thing from your mind. But it hasn't been quenched by the rain. You've just let yourself forget about it for the time being.

The same is true when a setback or a grueling day leaves you depressed and worried. You haven't lost your enthusiasm. You've simply let your mind focus on a disappointment or your weariness. If you were suddenly confronted with the chance to simply flip a switch and have what you most wanted in life, you'd quickly find the energy and resolve to do it. You'd instantly be able to tap your enthusiasm.

When you decide to create enthusiasm in less drastic circumstances, you're not fooling yourself either. You are fully aware of what you're doing, and you're doing it for a purpose you understand completely. You're getting in touch with a side of yourself that exists outside the moment in time you currently occupy. It's a side of yourself that defines who you are and what you want. It's utterly real.

Here are some ways to teach yourself how to be in touch with that abiding, defining self and all your enthusiasm for your objective.

Triggers. A trigger is a key word or phrase that reminds you of why you have enthusiasm. It should be closely associated with your major purpose. When you feel the need for an enthusiasm booster, think or say the word, and focus your mind on all that it means.

You'll dramatically strengthen the power of your triggers if you think of them when you find enthusiasm welling up on its own. Repeat the triggers, aloud or in your mind, in the midst of enthusiasm, and you'll reinforce the bond between the triggers and your feelings.

Some good triggers follow, but feel free to choose your own. Make them words that resonate for you and remind you that you will achieve success:

Action!
Drive!
Strength!
Desire!
I can!
I will!
On fire!
Onward!

Notice that each suggested trigger appears with an exclamation point. That's to remind you of the emphasis you should give the trigger when you use it. Think or say it forcefully, and you'll begin to feel enthusiasm with the same force.

Tokens. Choose some item that you have with you always, or which is always nearby. When you're feeling enthusiastic, handle or look at that item. Invest it with an association with your enthusiasm. If possible, touch it, so that the feeling of the item in your hands becomes tied to your enthusiasm.

This is a great way to bond your enthusiasm to something intimately associated with the work you're doing to achieve success. Every time you handle this token, you'll get a boost of enthusiasm.

Tokens can strike some people as childish, but they are very effective tools when used for a purpose. Anyone who has ever been a smoker can tell you how closely a cigarette becomes tied to certain actions or moods. Often, one of the hardest parts of quitting is breaking the association between a cigarette and something else satisfying. But instead of hobbling yourself with a negative bond such as smoking, you can create a positive association that will bolster your good feelings.

I can suggest some items that make good tokens, but feel free to be creative in choosing yours. What's important is that you pick an item that's always nearby.

A paperweight
Your glasses
A coin
A book
Your watch
A letter opener
A photograph

It's possible that some of these items might already be imbued with meaning for you. That's great. Take advantage of positive associations. If something has been given to you by a mentor you admire, it makes an excellent token. The same holds for something that symbolizes your goal. It could be a model, an award you've won, or a tool that is part of your job. A doctor could make a token of a stethoscope, an architect might choose a straight edge, and a caterer could use a whisk. Even if the item seems mundane now, you can make it highly significant.

Timing. Here's an amazingly useful approach that can help you ride out some of the roughest parts of the day. We all have routines or patterns in our daily lives. Those patterns include peaks of energy as well as troughs. One very common low point comes in the mid-afternoon, either just after lunch or about 4 o'clock, when our bodies are most likely to suggest that now would be a good time for a nap. Your low point may come at another time. It doesn't matter. The technique works whenever you apply it.

Choose a time when you want to feel enthusiasm. Make sure that you're near a clock or are wearing a watch so that your actions become associated with that specific time. (Alternatively, you can key your enthusiasm to a particular routine action.) Now, every day for two weeks, use either a trigger phrase or a token to tap into your enthusiasm. The only thing you have to do with your enthusiasm at this point is to make sure you associate it with the time you've chosen, although I'm sure you'll find plenty of things to apply it to.

It probably won't take the whole two weeks for the enthusiasm to become an ingrained response to the time (or action). But two full weeks of consciously creating enthusiasm under this specific circumstance will firmly establish the behavior in you.

To be enthusiastic, act enthusiastic.

This enthusiasm booster really works! The possibilities are almost unlimited. You can time it so that you greet your spouse in a great mood, attend meetings in top form, or even hit the gym ready to work hard. And if you're using it at a time of day when other people's enthusiasm tends to be flagging, like the after-lunch doldrums, you'll be a standout.

Action. One maxim that Napoleon Hill relished was this: to be enthusiastic, act enthusiastic.

By this, he meant that you can create enthusiasm by embracing its outward signs. That is, if you adopt the physical attributes of enthusiasm, you'll begin to feel enthusiastic. Again, this isn't fakery. You won't create enthusiasm where none exists. But you'll connect to your underlying feelings if you give them room for expression.

Here are some outward manifestations of enthusiasm in a person:

1. A smile
2. An upbeat tone of voice
3. Good posture
4. Positive language and an optimistic outlook
5. Looking others in the eye
6. Interest in the other person or persons
7. A sense of humor

These will be addressed in detail in an upcoming chapter, but for the moment, simply be aware that the lack of any of these puts a real damper on how other people perceive your enthusiasm, as well as how you feel yourself. Can you imagine convincing someone of something while frowning? While mumbling and looking at the floor? Of course not.

When you're feeling a lack of enthusiasm, adopt all the behaviors above. You can take them one at a time if you want. Get three or four of them down, and the others will probably happen automatically. You can't smile without seeming upbeat. You can't be interested in someone else without looking at them as they speak. They're all part and parcel of what happens when you're enthusiastic.

THE POWER OF ENTHUSIASTIC ACTION

One of the darkest moments of the reign of England's Queen Elizabeth I came when the Spanish Armada, at that time the greatest navy in the world, threatened to land upon England's shores. Spain was a great power, and England was then just a minor player in European affairs. Elizabeth's popularity among her subjects was shaky, and her army and navy were insufficient to oppose the Spanish.

Recognizing the importance of demonstrating her faith in her people and her cause, Elizabeth clad herself in gleaming white armor, mounted a white horse, and rode from London down to the fields where the greatest Spanish forces were expected. Her actions galvanized people all along her route, and when she arrived at the likely battlefield, she was greeted with tremendous cheers and excitement. The English people's determination to fight for their homeland was greater than ever.

Storms at sea made sure that few of the Spanish invaders ever made it to England. Even fewer made it ashore. In a sense, Elizabeth's display of enthusiasm was unnecessary. But stories of her daring and her determination swept around the countryside and around Europe. Her popularity at home surged, and for the rest of her reign, no European power dared contemplate an assault upon her realm.

This conscious, deliberate choice to act in an enthusiastic manner is no gimmick. It's just as honest as an unbidden feeling because it's a way of accessing feelings that are important to you. You aren't deceiving anyone. You're only making sure that the emotions you want to display are being given a means of expression.

> **Enthusiasm is useful in nearly any situation.**

No matter what methods you decide to use to create enthusiasm, you'll discover how valuable it is to have this energy and mental resolve at your beck and call. Be deliberate and aware of how you use your enthusiasm, but never fear to call upon it when you feel the need.

TIMING IS EVERYTHING

What, you may ask, should I do with all this enthusiasm now that I have it? When should I turn it on?

Enthusiasm is useful in nearly any situation. The following are examples of how you can apply it. These examples will be broad ones. After all, your major purpose is unlike anyone else's, and your circumstances will be unique:

Before you read your statement of purpose in the morning. Reading your statement of purpose will likely give you a jolt of enthusiasm on its own. However, if you take a few moments to make yourself enthusiastic before you begin reading, you'll reap a double dividend. You'll be more excited and more energized. And if this is the way you begin your morning, you'll find that your enthusiasm will color everything else you do.

Before you have a meeting. "Meeting" is used in a very general sense here. If you spend all day on the phone, then awaken your enthusiasm before you make your calls. If you're a salesperson, you'll probably have lots of meetings. But keep in mind that enthusiasm is a very convincing quality in a person. No matter whether you're trying to sell something or providing a service, you'll find people more receptive to you when you convey enthusiasm. You'll approach the encounter with more self-confidence, you'll enjoy it more, and you'll be more pleased with the result.

When you're avoiding something. We all have things we don't want to do, from work responsibilities to household chores. If there's a job you've been putting off, the best way to make sure you complete it is to begin in an enthusiastic state of mind. If you can't summon enthusiasm from your usual source, look for another method. Someone I know cleans the house while listening to dance music. It makes her want to move, sets a pace that she can follow, and injects some fun into a boring job.

When you meet someone negative. There are plenty of people out there who love to complain, to make gloomy predictions, and to share the unpleasantness they feel inside. The best advice, of course, is to avoid people like that as much as you can, but that isn't always possible. So, if you're stuck around someone whose attitude is negative, counter it with some enthusiasm. You can direct your enthusiasm to a task you share or simply funnel it into your own attitude. Most people with a negative outlook can't tolerate that. They may leave, or at least they'll stop complaining so they can avoid having you brighten up their terrible day. Do them a favor and be enthusiastic anyway.

When you stumble. Your attitude toward a setback is what makes it temporary or permanent. You can't ignore bad news, but you can decide to react to the situation it presents with enthusiasm. This doesn't mean celebrating. It does mean believing that there is a course of action available to you in which you can make choices and influence what happens next. Complete recovery may not be an immediate possibility, but if you enthusiastically believe that you can learn something important about what befell you, then you've already begun to tilt things back into your favor.

When you succeed. Take time to savor successes. Enjoy the way you feel. If you associate that feeling with trigger words and tokens, those will become even more powerful and effective for you. Here's one situation where proper control is very important, though. If you start to gloat, you're likely to feel self-important. You'll probably also irritate some people, which won't help your cause either.

When others stumble. Someone who has just suffered defeat is in need of a boost. You need to be diplomatic about sharing enthusiasm; you don't want to appear pitying. But expressing confidence in someone's ability to pick himself or herself up and go on may be all that person needs to hear in order to do just that. You'll be giving yourself a demonstration of just how useful enthusiasm is, while doing a good deed in the process.

When others succeed. When someone you know accomplishes something, give them enthusiastic, sincere acknowledgment. You are likely to do this automatically with people who are close to you, but there is no harm in offering a good word to someone you don't know well. Keeping your eyes open for opportunities like this is

Feeling enthusiasm course through your mind and body fundamentally alters your approach to any situation.

also a great personal morale booster. It's a way to remind yourself of the possibility of success and of sharing in the good feelings all around.

Enthusiasm is a personal miracle that you can create for yourself any time you need it. Feeling enthusiasm course through your mind and body fundamentally alters your approach to any situation. Like any powerful effect, it needs proper direction and control, but guided well, it will lift you up even when you feel you've never been so far down before.

There is no better way to begin any task before you than with enthusiasm. And there is no better fuel for the fires of enthusiasm than the satisfaction that comes from knowing that you can complete any goal you set for yourself. From your major purpose to your muddy entry-hall floor that needs to be mopped: each kind of task will be sooner done and less intimidating when you begin and complete it with enthusiasm.

Chapter 6

Surviving Disappointment

"No one can keep you down except yourself."

—Napoleon Hill

Tragedies, setbacks, and failures are a part of human existence. There is no absolute protection from them, and they can strike blows that seem to undo everything you've dreamed of and worked for. But they can also be overcome. You can attain success in spite of—and often because of—events that initially appear to be nothing short of devastating.

Triumphing over adversity isn't simply a matter of positive thinking. It requires persistence, grit, hard work, hard thinking, and a willingness to expose yourself to risk and hurt all over again. It can be painful, but the rewards can be great as well.

TURNING THE WHEEL

The poets tell us that the wheel of fortune is always turning, raising some people up while dragging others down. This is a good reminder that things happen to us that are beyond our control. But poetry and poets, to my mind, have always been a little too negative. Maybe this is because lots of poetry gets written when people are feeling wounded in the heart. I'll take Wordsworth's daffodils over lovesick moping any day. There's something about finding joy and beauty in the world that is much better for the spirit than pessimism.

> "Inside every defeat there is the seed of an equal or greater reward."

Heartbreak and pain are inevitable in life. But what isn't inevitable is how you respond to them. You can turn a disappointment into something lasting and beautiful. You can convert bad news into something useful and positive. It can be something very valuable to you.

Napoleon Hill wrote that "inside every defeat there is the seed of an equal or greater reward." Just what this reward is may not be clear when the world seems to fall apart around you, but it's there. No matter how devastating something seems in the first moments, it can become valuable, important, and helpful to you. A defeat can be a crushing blow you live with forever, if you let it, or it can be something you overcome and profit from.

This seems counterintuitive and hard to accept. We've all experienced losses and defeats, and it can be hard to believe that these events can be positive things. But let me demonstrate what I mean.

TURNAROUND TIME

Some think there's something overly sentimental about an affection for the book and movie *Gone with the Wind*.

They think it's a melodramatic story, and its heroine, Scarlett O'Hara is petty, selfish, manipulative, and dishonest. They're right about this.

But Scarlett is a powerful heroine. She never gives up. Fate, the Yankees, or her own foolish schemes are always humiliating her, impoverishing her, or embarrassing her. Yet she never fails to pick herself up, look for a new goal, and start going after it.

> When you take the time to see what your error has been, you're in a much better position to recover from it.

Scarlett is deeply flawed as a human being. She sabotages many of her own best efforts. She throws away love, makes others miserable, and can't even begin to see what she is doing to them.

She doesn't learn from her mistakes, but she does move beyond them. You can do both. When you take the time to see what your error has been, you're in a much better position to recover from it.

So, if the only lesson you learn from Scarlett is this, you'll be ready to recover from any disappointment you encounter: tomorrow is another day.

Because we all experience so much negative thinking in the course of our lives, it's often easier to conclude that a good thing can be a bad thing in disguise than it is to trust that a bad thing is really something positive. Here's one obvious example of the first case: A woman wins the lottery. That's swell, until she discovers she doesn't know how to handle sudden wealth. She outspends her new income, her family falls apart over fights about money, and she acquires new habits and new personality traits that make herself and everybody who knows her miserable.

Another woman gets the promotion she's been working for over the past decade. She has the salary, position, and respect she's always dreamed of having. But suddenly, her colleagues are jealous, she has less time for her family, and her work time is taken up by administrative responsibilities she dislikes. Gradually, her dream job turns into a nightmare.

If good things can turn bad, why then, is it hard to accept that things that seem bad can, in truth, be good? Because negative mental programming gives us the idea that the world is more likely to offer bad things than good. This is an unfounded belief. It's not a fact. It's a harmful, limiting, defeatist idea.

People who accept the idea that it is up to us to determine whether something is ultimately good or bad understand three important points. First, they realize that there is a choice being made. We choose, consciously and wholeheartedly, to determine our reactions to events. We don't simply respond to news; we evaluate it and judge its implications and its causes. Then, we decide how to act.

Second, we realize that our choice of reactions will profoundly affect whether we'll succeed or fail. We know that no matter how disappointing or frightening an event is, we can extract something from it that will make us stronger, wiser, or happier. We don't have to like or enjoy everything we encounter. But we are determined that we'll shape it and that it won't determine everything that happens to us.

And, third, we understand that any defeat or any set-back is only temporary as long as we choose to rise above it. We can choose to put a mistake behind us. We can choose to find out what caused a defeat and make the necessary corrections. We can choose to remember that as long as we have the powers of our mind at our disposal, we still possess the essential tools to learn from defeat and put our life back on course.

These choices require strength, determination, and, above all, PMA. But they are our choices, and we're resolved to make them as we see fit—morally, purposefully, and powerfully. We make our own success. We achieve what we want in life. We change the world in ways large and small.

Harriet Tubman was born a slave. She was legally the property of another person, with no say in where she lived or how she worked. She could have accepted that situation, but she rejected it. After escaping slavery, she brought hundreds of people to freedom herself and inspired thousands of more slaves to escape through the Underground Railroad. She wasn't imprisoned by her lost freedom and the oppression of her people. She opposed those hardships and disadvantages her entire life and set an example of leadership that endures many years later.

Helen Keller was blind and deaf. It took years before Anne Sullivan broke through the isolation in which Keller lived. But once she was aware that the barriers around her could be overcome, Keller was determined to help others overcome them as well. Through writings and appearances, as well as by making herself an example, she transformed society's ideas about what was possible for people without vision and hearing. Today, the blind and

Pain and suffering are fuel for struggle. the deaf are part of society in ways that were unimaginable when Helen Keller was a child.

Obstacles can also be inspirations. Barriers are signs to new pathways. Pain and suffering are fuel for struggle. The things these women achieved weren't accidents. Their successes were the result of the thoughts and actions of people who would not let adversity stand in their way.

TAKING HOLD OF THE WHEEL

Inspiration is powerful. It can carry you forward when everything else seems to have fallen away. Although there's no simple formula for coping with disaster and pain, you can begin, even when things seem their darkest, to lay the groundwork for your recovery.

First, recognize that your defeat is temporary. If you are alive, you can recover. You can be stronger and wiser for the knowledge you'll gain, and, as your recovery progresses, become aware that you have an ability to bounce back that has never been tested.

A jolt early on in your plan for success can teach you a lesson. You can come to understand that all the qualities that made it possible for you to plan for success are still there. They are inside of you. These qualities are a result of your own mind—the one thing you can always control—and you can use them for anything you want.

As a second step, give yourself some time to absorb and accept the specifics of what has happened to you. In most psychological models of grieving, denial is a common step. But denial is something you can't afford. The sooner you come to grips with what you've experienced, the better.

Try, though, not to characterize what's happened to you too strongly. It's fine to admit that you're disappointed, hurt, shocked, unhappy, or frightened. Your emotional response is valid,

> **Be deliberate about separating your feelings from your analysis of what went wrong.**

and you'll have to deal with it. But for the moment, resist the temptation to let your initial feelings tell you what is going to happen next. It's far too easy to decide that because one thing has gone wrong, everything else will too. This just stops you in your tracks when what you need to do is start moving again.

You'll need to be clear-eyed about what your disappointments mean to you. Sometimes they reveal a loss caused by someone else; sometimes they reveal a mistake in your own thinking. It can be much easier to accept the revelation of one's own mistake as an obvious benefit, even though that realization can be humbling. When you're confronting a setback that is caused by your own misjudgment, though, you need to be deliberate about separating your feelings from your analysis of what went wrong.

Artists are a good example of people for whom this kind of separation is keenly important. Often, the failure of a work or idea is intimately connected with an artist's idea of himself or herself. If artists can't separate a bad performance from their identity, they'll be trapped in their pain and run the risk of self-pity.

When you're working for your definite purpose, a setback can hurt you as deeply as it can any artist. You need to be as professional and determined as any actor who ever got bad reviews and went on to turn in an Academy Award-winning performance. Your personal Oscar depends on taking a good hard look at why you made a mistake and then deciding how to correct it. The correction may involve a small change, or it may take a huge readjustment. You are capable of either.

Once you know how you need to retune your plan for success, take some time to deal with your feelings about the mistake. Recognize that making a mistake doesn't mean that you are always hasty, timid, uninspired, careless, or whatever it is that you think tripped you up. You may have some tendencies in your behavior that you need to modify. If that's the case, begin immediately to make the changes in your behavior. Don't dwell on your belief that you are somehow flawed.

PMA is very important to keeping your mind focused on what you can accomplish. You can change your behavior. You can achieve your goal. You can use PMA to do both, and you'll begin to succeed at it as soon as you start trying.

ELIMINATING THE CAUSES OF FAILURE

Some people can never accept responsibility for their own mistakes. I doubt you're one of those people. If you were, it would never occur to you to try to modify your behavior by reading a book like this. Still, it's possible that the source of your temporary setback is something you haven't considered until it leaves you hurt and baffled. The following list of reasons for failure was adapted from a list that Napoleon Hill devised. It's not exhaustive, but it should give you some things to think about.

1. Lack of a purpose in life
2. Lack of necessary education
3. Lack of ambition
4. Lack of persistence and follow-through*
5. Lack of self-confidence*
6. Lack of tolerance for other people
7. Lack of imagination*
8. Lack of a budget for money and time*
9. Lack of self-discipline*
10. Desire for revenge
11. Desire for quick and easy success
12. Negative Mental Attitude

You have the power to change anything about your behavior that stands in the way of your major purpose. One very effective way to begin making the change is to draw on the ideas from the previous lesson. If you can make

---

* These are dealt with in later chapters. If you're truly convinced that one of these causes is behind a disappointment you've faced, resolve on the spot to begin eliminating that characteristic from your behavior.

yourself enthusiastic, you can make yourself more motivated, more self-confident, more honest, more tolerant, or anything else you need to be to succeed.

The trigger, token, and timing techniques can all be used to stimulate yourself to engage in the new behavior you want. More important, the action technique is a highly effective vehicle for making sure you are practicing the new behavior you've chosen.

> **You don't want to create a spectacular spiral of disappointments for yourself by living in the past.**

These first three techniques are also useful for stopping yourself when you begin to brood about a temporary failure. Once you've recognized any role you played in your setback and identified how you're going to correct things, you won't help yourself by obsessing over old errors. If you choose to relive unfortunate decisions, you'll undermine your PMA and just set yourself up to repeat the old mistakes and make new ones. You don't want to create a spectacular spiral of disappointments for yourself by living in the past.

Closing the door on the past doesn't mean that you're pretending this error didn't happen. It doesn't mean that you aren't responsible for the consequences either. It means, plainly and simply, that you've resolved that this single event won't define you. You've determined that it won't limit you, stop you, or control you. You are activating the powers of your mind—your single-greatest, most powerful asset—to choose who you are and what you are doing.

No matter how hard you work, you can't completely insulate yourself from disappointments, and maybe that's not such a bad thing. Setbacks and limitations can be transformed into something new and wonderful when you decide you're in control.

There will be sadness and pain in your life, no matter how carefully you plan. You'll meet with defeat perhaps as often as you know the thrill of success. But you, and only you, have the power to determine which of these feelings drives your actions. Remember that anything that happens to you can eventually inspire you into taking steps to reach your definite major purpose.

Chapter 7

Staying the Course

"Think before you act and save the time you would otherwise devote to correcting mistakes."

—Napoleon Hill

We all experience times when we seem to lose our focus. We know what we're capable of accomplishing, but the time just doesn't seem to be there, nor the energy. Sometimes we add just one more thing to our agenda, and everything we're doing starts to spiral out of control. When something interrupts your flow of work, you need to recognize it and apply some good old-fashioned self-discipline.

Self-discipline. There's a concept that smacks of starvation diets, grim asceticism, and a sense of humor that runs the gamut from A to A. You probably first heard the word intoned as a child, when an adult sternly tried to impress upon you the importance of something like doing your homework or keeping your room clean. It's tied up with a sense of denial or duty. It's required in order to satisfy other people.

But these are wrong impressions. Self-discipline is a tool that you use for your own benefit. You apply it to get

something you want. You don't use it to engage in unpleasant activities. It doesn't make you dull or unhappy.
It creates time for yourself and **Strengthen your**
what you want in life. It brings **self-discipline,**
you satisfaction, peace of mind, **and you'll have**
and control over all the demands **more enthusiasm,**
that you face. Self-discipline **fewer setbacks,**
makes all your efforts pay off in **and more vibrant**
benefits that bring you closer to **PMA.**
your goals.

Self-discipline is liberating and exciting. It's the manifestation of the control you have over the way you think.
Apply self-discipline, and you'll see your list of unfulfilled
responsibilities shrink until you're ready for new ones.
Strengthen your self-discipline, and you'll have more enthusiasm, fewer setbacks, and more vibrant PMA. It's a
tremendous tool for enhancing all the qualities you've
been cultivating in yourself.

The wonderful thing is, if you start small, it will grow
on its own. You don't have to tackle the most overwhelming issues first. You can begin with baby steps and find
that you're making huge strides before you know it.

THE TWO-FOLD PATH

You must apply self-discipline in two realms: your actions and your emotions. Each area affects the other, to
differing degrees, in each individual. But for almost everyone, emotions are both the key and the trap. Let them
run away with you, and you'll lose all control over your

actions. It's true that thoughtless actions can send you into emotional upheaval, but with a firm grip on how you allow your emotions to influence your actions, you won't have to worry as much about what you're physically doing.

This book began by encouraging you to develop PMA precisely because it's a form of emotional self-discipline. When your mental attitude is upbeat and confident, you're not giving less attractive emotions any room in your mind or your heart. All the affirmations that you use to create and sustain PMA lay the groundwork for emotional self-discipline. Assuming that you've been working on PMA for a while now, it's time to examine some other forms of mental self-discipline.

To do this, we'll examine what Napoleon Hill identified as the fourteen major emotions that arise in all of us when we encounter the appropriate stimuli:

Positive Emotions	Negative Emotions
a. Love	a. Hatred
b. Sex	b. Jealousy
c. Hope	c. Fear
d. Loyalty	d. Revenge
e. Enthusiasm	e. Anger
f. Faith	f. Superstition
g. Desire	g. Greed

I've juggled the order of Hill's list to point out some obvious connections between certain emotions. Any emotion can develop into its opposite. This is both bad and good. Bad because undisciplined positive emotions can transform into something ugly. Good because you have the power to turn a negative emotional reaction into something useful and beneficial.

There's nothing wrong at all with experiencing any of these emotions. We all get angry or frightened; we all feel a twinge of jealousy or hatred. If you feel a negative emotion, it's very important that you don't deny it or repress it. It will only burrow into your mind and grow stronger. The positive emotions must also be acknowledged for what they are.

Emotional self-discipline requires two things of you: recognition and assertion. You have to begin with recognition. Asserting control is impossible if you don't know what you're trying to control. So, when an emotion comes along, don't clamp down on it right away. Give a name to it without making a judgment about it. If you're experiencing conflicting emotions, which is a real possibility, the sooner you admit to feeling one, the sooner you'll be able to identify the other feelings as well.

It may be immediately obvious to you why you're feeling as you are. Some emotions are triggered by familiar events or relationships. But we all have a tendency to avoid admitting the existence or the cause of some emotional states because another emotion comes into play: fear.

Admitting that you have certain feelings can be frightening because it suggests that you aren't in control of your emotions. A physical passion for someone who, for whatever reason, isn't an appropriate choice, is a good example of this. It can be very disturbing to be attracted to someone who is off-limits, and it can quickly lead you to doubt your wisdom, your goodness, or even your sanity. In response to a threat like this, you may be tempted to bury your sexual feelings under your fear. You actually strengthen your fear in order to combat your sexual urges. No matter what other emotions you may feel toward the person who attracts you, you let fear become the dominant state. But your recognition of emotions needs to be nonjudgmental initially. Otherwise, you won't be able to get an accurate fix on how you're feeling. And without that recognition, you can't move on to the next step: assertion.

Assertion begins at the point where you choose to act based on your emotional state. This applies to any of the emotions, positive or negative. You can make several useful choices at this point:

1. You can choose to act on the emotion in a thoughtful, measured way.
2. You can choose to adapt your emotional response before acting.
3. You can choose to wait to do either.

Generally speaking, it's best if you choose #1 for positive emotions and #2 for negative emotions. But it's very easy to imagine exceptions to both cases. When it comes to acting, remember that emotions such as love and sex are powerful, and we spent an entire chapter learning about the pros and cons of enthusiasm. Similarly, it can sometimes be essential to acknowledge and act on negative emotions. Fear can hold you back, but it can also keep you out of a dark alleyway. Anger is an appropriate response in some situations, as long as your display of that anger isn't excessive.

Adapting your emotional response also requires careful consideration. You need to be confident in your ability to channel your emotions into new pathways. This requires practice and self-knowledge. You don't want to disregard an entirely appropriate feeling. And you need to be sure that you are truly changing your response, not hiding it from yourself.

As for choice #3, this isn't an act of repression; it's a judgment call you make based on your assessment of your capacity to accomplish either of the two choices above. You're not avoiding a hot topic; you're giving yourself time to gain perspective. Powerful emotions can sometimes be extremely temporary. They can be triggered by associations that have little to do with the matter at hand. But you shouldn't use this choice as an avoidance mechanism. You must take the first opportunity to examine your feelings and their sources.

THE CONSIDERED EMOTION

Exercising self-discipline when it comes to positive emotions may seem like a joyless, calculating action, but, actually, an emotion that is expressed consciously and with thoughtful awareness is given its best and truest expression. You can commit to it without hesitation once you know that you want to act on the emotion and know how to do it best.

Love is the emotion that many people feel is held back too often. It's common to hear people lament that the words "I love you" aren't spoken enough in this world. That particular point is true, but there is a more important truth: love is most meaningful when it's fully acknowledged and expressed deliberately.

This isn't to say that impulsive expressions of emotions are out of place in a self-disciplined mind. You can feel the urge to hug someone, tell them a joke, or say a prayer, and then act on that urge. When you've begun to exercise self-discipline, you'll know in that split second whether the urge you feel is the right one to act on. In fact, because you gain so much self-knowledge through enforcing self-discipline, you may actually find yourself feeling freer to be more expressive.

How, then, do you know when your emotional response should be translated into action, and how do you choose that action? Emotional clarity derives from self-discipline. You'll understand what you're feeling and why. You'll then be in the position to ask yourself the following:

1. Is my expression welcome?
2. Will it convey what I want it to?
3. Will it help me?

While it may be appropriate sometimes to express an emotion that is contrary to what other people are doing and thinking, you need to make that decision in full awareness of the reaction it will inspire. A hug may fluster someone who isn't as physically expressive as you are. Laughter might make other people think you aren't serious.

If you do choose to give an expression that isn't welcomed, you need to be sure of hitting the second point. Maybe laughter will shock someone, but it might get them to pay attention to something they've ignored. An expression of concern about an idea or behavior can be very unwelcome, but if it makes an important point, then it can be worthwhile. However, if you sense that you aren't going to get your point across, it's better to hold back. You can choose a more effective means of expressing your feelings at another point.

As for helping yourself, there are many advantages to be gained from expressing your feelings. You can simply gain the satisfaction of letting someone else know how you feel. You can promote your agenda for attaining your objective. You can resolve ambiguities in business as well as personal relationships. Having a clear sense of where you're going and what you want to achieve is essential for exercising self-discipline. You simply shouldn't make a decision without some idea of how to evaluate what will happen. If you do, you won't know whether any possible bad reactions are worth the possible gains. You won't even be able to tell if any reaction is good or bad for you. And why, you wonder, would you make a choice that didn't help you? Because it helps someone else.

That person can be your child or spouse, a colleague, or a stranger on the street. You can do something that has no hint of a reward for yourself as long as you know that it will be beneficial to someone who needs it.

The point here is that a considered response to an emotion is a worthy one. As you adopt this strategy, you'll find yourself more in tune with how you feel. You'll learn to understand your feelings better and to be confident that you're expressing them in ways that are good and helpful. Self-discipline truly defines you more clearly as the person you want to become.

A considered response to an emotion is a worthy one.

ACTIONS THAT SPEAK

Another area where self-discipline is important is your daily activity. When you're making decisions about your work and your responsibilities, you need those decisions to produce effective results. When you apply self-discipline on a routine basis, it will make you more capable, more constructive, and more successful in meeting your short- and long-term goals.

We all enjoy some parts of our daily routine more than others. There is a natural tendency to favor actions that are pleasurable over those that seem like chores. Maybe you like making a sale, but filling out a report form is drudgery. The time you spend talking with your kids flies by, but checking on their homework leaves you cold.

That's fine. It's only human. There's nothing wrong with feeling that way. However, if you let your feelings control your actions, you'll slip into trouble. Work that you put off never goes away. A stack of incomplete reports is much more daunting than a single form, especially when your boss is screaming for them.

The key, of course, is to make uninteresting jobs something you do automatically. A report gets written as soon as you have all the information you need. Strong self-discipline is usually a matter of exerting a small, extra amount of control at a key moment. There are several easy ways to accomplish this.

Structure. Arrange your activities so that something you dislike is immediately followed by an activity that you enjoy. A completed sales report can give you permission to move on to a new sales call. You can be creative with this. Just make sure that the reward is something positive and useful.

You may have arranged your daily routine in an opposite manner to what I've suggested. It's common to start the day off with things you enjoy and push all the unpleasant jobs to the end, in the hopes that the day will fill up, giving you an excuse to avoid the task. Altering your usual work patterns can seem disruptive at first, but if you persevere for just a couple of days, you'll start feeling more in control. You'll enjoy not having something hanging over your head all the time. While a stack of unfinished reports sits on your desk as a silent reproach, a file full of completed reports can become a signal of productivity.

Making these minor adjustments will become easier as you strengthen your self-discipline. While it's still young and tender, however, you can use a technique that you're already familiar with.

Sparks. A spark is really the same as a trigger or an affirmation. It's a word or a phrase that you invest with meaning. You think or say the word when you feel tempted to avoid something that must be done, and it gives you the push you need to apply yourself.

One obvious spark is a phrase from Napoleon Hill: Do it now! This one is direct, powerful, and suited to just about any circumstance. As you identify areas where you feel the need to apply self-discipline, you can create sparks of your own. Keep them short. Make them commanding. You never have to tell anyone what they are, either, so you can make them utterly personal. Here's a list of sparks designed to give you some inspiration for your own choices:

Spark	Purpose
Ten more minutes!	Great for completing any task
Smile!	Keeps your mood positive
Listen and Learn!	Focuses your mind when someone is boring you
Over and Done!	Another boost to complete something
I win!	Reminds you of how you benefit
My choice!	Focuses your attention on the fact that you're doing something you know is needed
Healthier and Happier!	Good for resisting urges to harm yourself by eating or drinking too much, or by smoking

You can create sparks to suit almost any need. The more often you use them, the stronger they'll be. Some of the affirmations and triggers you've already selected may work very well as sparks. Words or phrases that do double duty for you are always potent.

Words or phrases that do double duty for you are always potent.

Most of the time, when you get the little details in order, you'll find that the bigger picture begins to take care of itself. That's because self-discipline is a habit. Give it a little room in your life, and self-discipline will expand into every area. The same is true of avoidance. If you discover that you're shying away from something that needs to be done, work quickly to nip that new habit in the bud. You don't want to give yourself the message that it's okay to neglect responsibilities. Make determined action a habit, and it will simplify your life.

Make determined action a habit, and it will simplify your life.

THE INTEGRATED PERSON

Self-discipline makes sure that you can work on the things you've decided are important. It readies you for new opportunities, helps you over the bumps in the day, and gives you peace of mind. Self-discipline is so much more than saying no to an extra helping of pasta. It's creating behaviors that make the things you value in life possible.

In a way, self-discipline encapsulates everything that goes into Napoleon Hill's principles of success. Once you realize that you can direct your thoughts and emotions, using the only thing you can control—your mind—directing your actions is much easier.

Begin small if you need to. Choose the simplest thing that you tend to avoid, and give yourself a few days to understand how empowering it can be to gain control over that ugly detail. The chance to move on to something more important will be waiting for you as soon as you realize what you're capable of.

You're building the world you want to live in, one step at a time.

And if you stumble, don't despair. Begin again. The memory of a minor setback may be all it takes to stiffen your backbone the next time. You're not creating perfection. You're building the world you want to live in, one step at a time.

Chapter 8

Taking Some Risks

Extending yourself into new territories where you need new skills and new ideas, and where the rewards are visible but uncertain, means opening yourself up to defeat. It can mean losing money, prestige, freedom, and power. It isn't easy.

But it is essential.

You've already taken some risks. Just by reading this book—even if you haven't yet acted on a thing you've read—you've risked exposing yourself to ideas that will make you think differently. You're no longer going to view yourself and what you're capable of accomplishing in the same way. You won't be satisfied with the status quo anymore. You're going to want to change things and try new ways of thinking.

And changes expose you to disruptions and setbacks. Other people may laugh at you or scorn you. A situation that seemed just fine will now seem confining and unrewarding.

But risks bring rewards.

If you've begun applying what you've learned in this book, you're already more positive and confident. You have a new sense of possibilities, as well as a goal that you've defined and created a plan for achieving. Those things alone make life more exciting and rewarding, even if you haven't accomplished the first item in your plan for success.

But the great reward—your major purpose—will require more risks. Achieving it will mean that you have to go out on a limb, be vulnerable, and overcome defeats. No one ever achieves what they want in life without taking some risks—and no one wins every single time.

However, there are ways that you can stack the odds in your favor. You don't need to cheat, either. The only thing you have to do is understand the house rules when it comes to risk-taking. And, in this case, the house isn't a Las Vegas casino. It's the universe itself.

Yes, there are rules for placing your bets in life and rules that govern the payoffs you'll take home. They aren't as neatly defined as the rules at a blackjack table, but then again, they aren't set up to favor the house either. The universe's rules are fair and just. They apply whether you know them or not. But with knowledge of how they work, you can use them to place your bets at the right table at the right time.

COSMIC CONSISTENCY

What kind of world do we live in?

If you stand on a street corner in a big city and ask that question of the people going by, you're likely to get as many different answers as the number of times you ask the question. Most of the answers will be colored by what has been happening to the respondents. Their ideas will reflect frustration and hope, as well as optimism and despair. People will fumble to make a statement about the economy, express worry about war and ethnic conflict, or concern about the environment. There's likely to be some grumbling about the media and a few complaints about politics. A die-hard sports fan will likely update you on the state of the playoffs or the chances for next year.

But then suppose I pass by, and you ask me.

I'll look you in the eye, smile, and say something I learned from Napoleon Hill's teachings: "We live in a world where every action has not just one reaction, but infinite echoes. We live in a world that we shape by our thoughts and our deeds. We can make it a dark and hopeless place or one that is full of wonderful surprises and great rewards. The universe gives us what we prepare ourselves to get from it."

Could you prepare yourself to get the things you want from the world? Yes, you can. Change yourself, alter your thinking, and you'll start changing your life and the world. This happens because of the way your mind works and because of the very nature of the world itself.

I'm going to try to demonstrate the nature of our world to you, as envisioned by Napoleon Hill. These ideas may sound somewhat religious to you, but no matter what your particular faith may be, they aren't in conflict with the fundamental tenets of your own religion. All the great religions share an understanding of the nature of this world. That's what gives them their mass appeal. There are differences on many issues, but no major ones about the role we each play in shaping our lives. And if you're an agnostic or an atheist, let me assure you that this discussion won't center on a Supreme Being in whom you must believe.

The scientific understanding of the forces that govern the universe is incomplete and evolving. There are grand models and theories that physicists are struggling to prove. Discovery of a new particle here or proof of a new force there will go on for decades if not centuries.

But science, all science, is predicated on a belief that the world operates consistently. The rules that govern the behavior of quarks are the same in Chicago as they are in Bora Bora, on Earth, and on Saturn. The motion of the planets around the sun doesn't alter from Wednesday to Thursday, or stop altogether in even numbered years. Science tells us that the forces that determine both the movement and properties of subatomic particles, as well as of planets, are always the same.

This idea is what makes science possible. It lies at the root of the scientific method of testing and retesting, coming up with repeatable results in experiments to prove that a supposed cause leads to a given effect. This hasn't always been the way people understood the universe. Ancient cultures believed that gods moved the sun, caused the seasons, and made rivers flow. Apollo could veer his chariot of the sun closer to the earth and scorch the land. Now, even those with an abiding belief in a creator understand that the operation of the world, its mechanics, are orderly.

This doesn't diminish the wonder we feel at a beautiful sunset or when we stand on the shore and admire the power of the ocean. We understand that there are great forces at work, and though human perception of just how all those forces interact is still slight, we know that the color of the sky and the rhythm of the waves are a result of a consistent framework.

Napoleon Hill called this framework *Infinite Intelligence*; Infinite because it encompassed the whole of the universe, and Intelligence because it was so intricately and precisely constructed that it seemed to him to represent a profound awareness, that is, a unifying order to the cosmos.

A CONSISTENT WORLDVIEW

Focus on the idea of cosmic order. You can see that the physical world does behave in a consistent manner. The moon doesn't suddenly aim itself at the earth. You don't wake up in the morning wondering if the sun has risen, if gasoline will still ignite in the cylinders of car engines, or if 3 + 3 will still equal 6. These things are constant and unchanging.

That simple understanding is all you need to see that there is an enduring and coherent pattern to the world and how it operates. Here we're touching on *Cosmic Habit-force*, the final law discovered by Napoleon Hill, which will be addressed later in this book.

How, then, does this idea of an Infinite Intelligence affect you and your desire for success in life?

You can use this Infinite Intelligence to your advantage to manipulate the forces of the world—in ways consistent with how they always operate—to achieve your goals. Very simply, the structure of the universe itself is a tool that you can apply to your quest for your major purpose.

This is true whether you're a scientist or an engineer, a lawyer or a homemaker, a sales rep or an artist. And

I'm not talking about using a particle accelerator or re-inforced concrete. I'm talking about using Infinite Intelligence to change yourself and what you're capable of accomplishing. Understand how Infinite Intelligence works, and you'll know when you're ready to take the necessary risks.

APPLIED FAITH

When you accept that the universe operates consistently, the next step is to realize how often you already make choices on the assumption that it will continue to do so. Athletes do this when they train. They push themselves to greater efforts each day, knowing that the repeated exertion of effort will increase their skills and endurance. They might not express it in exactly those words, but they are staking everything on the idea that what has worked for them will continue to work. If they decided to add something different to their workout, or to stretch in a new way, they still believe that they will get results from their actions. Their training prepares them to do new things, reach new goals, and set new records.

To be ready to take the risks you need to take, you must understand how you've been training yourself with faith in Infinite Intelligence. Think of yourself like an athlete. Your training has been mental, not physical, but you've been toning your mind. You've pumped it up with PMA and stretched it out with enthusiasm. You've been working with people in your Master Mind group, testing your skills, and learning new moves. Learning from defeat has helped you focus on concentrated thinking and observation, so that you're mentally sharp and resilient.

But like an athlete, all the training in the world is useless unless you enter a competition. While sports players are out there vying with the best athletes in the world, your competition is only with yourself. You're trying to do better and go farther than the self who bought this book because you were unsatisfied with certain aspects of your life. You don't have to beat anyone's performance but your own. And then, once you establish a new personal best, you'll be ready to train yourself to do even better.

One important caveat about applied faith is that while it depends on optimism and determination, it also works within the framework of Infinite Intelligence. That is, applied faith doesn't mean that anything you want or need is possible simply because you want or need it. It means that you can achieve the things you make yourself ready to do. You can't assume that applied faith makes something possible that you're simply not ready to receive. If you need money for your plan, you won't get it simply by having faith that it will come. You'll find that money, however, if you train yourself to get it.

Let's say that you do need some cash—$10,000 is a nice, round sum. There are lots of ways to come up with it. Someone without applied faith might enter the lottery or start looking for a bag full of bills on the street. Although this is not likely to be successful, people are often as aimless as that.

But with applied faith, you might pursue a bank loan. You'd get an application, fill it out, and supply all the records necessary to prove that you were a worthwhile risk for the bank. And if the bank disagreed with you, you'd try other means. Another bank, a second mortgage, borrowing against your 401(k), or borrowing from a family member or friend. You would be out there trying, acting on the assumption that there was an honest, fair way to obtain the money. And you would not stop trying until you were successful.

Throughout your efforts, your mind would be positive, your mood enthusiastic. You might hear "no" several times, even many times, but you wouldn't give up. Along the way, you might learn a few things about why people are reluctant to lend to you, and you'd start correcting those deficiencies. Making changes like that would just be another form of preparing yourself for the money.

> **You only need to begin deliberately and repeatedly pushing yourself to do more than you have in the past.**

Keeping your mind in peak mental condition to apply the powers of Infinite Intelligence is, like athletic training, something that requires regular, conscious effort. But like a child who takes her first hesitant step on a balance beam years before she comes home from the Olympics a champion, you can begin getting in mental shape. You don't need special equipment. You don't have to get up before dawn and run five miles. You only need to begin deliberately and repeatedly pushing yourself to do more than you have in the past.

STRETCHING YOURSELF

You know where you've been holding back. We all have areas where we are less certain of ourselves. Some of us are nervous about money, others worry about independence. Where one person fears embarrassment, another is uncomfortable with making waves. But it's precisely in the areas where you feel least confident that you need to begin using applied faith. Remember that acting with applied faith means preparing yourself first. If you're shy about public speaking, don't stand up in front of a crowd first thing tomorrow. It's best to begin with small steps. The important thing is to begin.

Let's take the example of fear of public speaking. According to many surveys, it's a very common fear. Here are suggestions of how you might prepare yourself to take the risk of making a speech, which can show you how to prepare yourself to face any risk.

You've got two weeks to get ready to address a group of fifty people at work. Right now, the prospect knots your stomach. Begin by asking yourself if you'd have trouble talking to five people sitting around a table. Probably not; you've done it before. The informal setting is always less intimidating, even if you're talking to strangers. But this is an important realization. You've already spoken to a small group and done just fine. So, the size of your audience is part of what's troubling you.

Now ask yourself why fifty people are scarier than five. Do you feel uncertain about what you'll be saying? Do you think they'll be hostile to your points? Are you afraid that they'll think you're dull or stupid? This is where self-discipline is helpful. If you can identify your emotional responses, you'll have a clearer idea of what you need to deal with.

We'll assume that what you discover is that you believe you're going to fail due to a lack of preparation. You remember speech class in high school, how you never liked the topics you were assigned, how you wrote your speeches out on the school bus the morning they were due, how you skipped a page and everyone laughed, and how you got a lecture from the teacher on not being prepared.

Now we're getting somewhere. You're feeling like you're doomed to fail because you won't be prepared and you'll make mistakes.

But here's the truth: you can be prepared, and you can prevent mistakes.

You start by beginning your presentation right away. You don't try to make it the funniest speech anyone ever heard. You just take the time to get everything you need to say written down. You give yourself time to revise and check your facts. You even print the speech out in great big letters. Yes, some people can speak effectively from note cards. But you're a first timer and you want to get the details right.

Now you begin to practice. You tape yourself and listen to the speed of your voice, and decide that you tend to rush, so you insert extra spaces into your text just to slow your reading down. You discover some sentences that look fine on paper but don't sound as good when they're spoken aloud. You change them. You break them up into shorter sentences and get rid of words that you stumble over.

Then you stay late at work one evening and go to the room where you'll be speaking. You practice your speech there in the empty room, just listening to the sound of yourself speaking. You put your coat on one chair and your briefcase on another. As you speak, you don't always look down at your papers. You look up each time you read a sentence and focus your eyes on one of the chairs you've marked.

By now, you know your speech pretty well. It's only four minutes long. You decide to try it from memory. You don't get all the words right, but when your memory fails, you still know what you want to express, and you make your point.

And then it's the day of the speech. You pump yourself up with PMA. You're not wildly enthusiastic, but you're calm. You walk to the front of the room and begin. Your practice pays off. You make eye contact with your audience, you get all your points across, and even though you have to look down at your speech a couple of times, no one listening notices that, or cares, if they do.

When you're done, there aren't any cheers. But there aren't any boos either. The meeting goes on as it should.

And when it's done, you might even volunteer to do the same thing next time!

This is exactly how using applied faith works. You begin by deciding to succeed at a task. You then take full account of the obstacles in your way and methodically begin to address them. You devote time and effort beforehand. Applied faith depends on PMA. And you continue with a willingness to keep working even after the immediate goal is achieved.

Applied faith creates results in the physical world, but it begins its work in your mind. It's there that applied faith begins making changes in your thoughts and behavior that prepare you for the results you need. There's nothing mystical about the process, but it can sometimes accomplish more than you expect. While you're concentrating on one target, you prepare yourself for something greater and more beneficial that you might not even realize you need.

Eleanor Roosevelt began making public appearances for her husband, Franklin, after he contracted polio. She didn't enjoy giving speeches to political clubs, and she wasn't the likeliest speaker from a physical perspective. She was a plain woman, with a reedy voice. But she knew that public speaking was important to Franklin's political prospects and, just as important, to his realization that polio wouldn't mean the end of his public life. So, she worked hard at it and gained a measure of personal fame that was very unusual for a woman in that era.

Of course, Franklin did resume his political career and was elected president of the United States four times. Vaulted into the public eye in an entirely new way, Eleanor discovered she had a tremendous opportunity that she had never expected. She became an advocate for working people, women, and children, and spoke up on issues of public health and civil rights. Her positions were sometimes even at odds with her husband's administration, and she sometimes took on the job of pushing the government to do more for the people it had been ignoring. After Franklin's death, unlike any First Lady before, she remained in the public eye, serving as the American ambassador to the United Nations.

Eleanor Roosevelt didn't plan to become such a prominent figure in the days when she first began to practice her speeches. She had no idea where her path would lead her. But it presented her with an amazing opportunity, and when it came, she was prepared to seize it and do profound things.

> **Tackling a small thing can ready you for something much bigger.**

Unlike Eleanor, you have a plan. Your ambitions are your own. But applied faith can still help you; it can make you ready for challenges, both positive and negative, that you don't even know you'll face. Tackling a small thing can ready you for something much bigger, revealing skills you weren't aware of, opening doors that you never noticed, and tapping a personal strength that you've underestimated.

THE DARK SIDE

Applied faith also has a disturbing side. Simply put, if your faith is fixed on negative results, it will prepare you for them. Your work will produce frustration, bad news will accumulate faster than you can digest it, and you'll make yourself miserable.

This is one reason why it's important to maintain PMA. PMA leaves little mental room for faith in negative results. It's also why you should seriously attempt to understand the causes of any setbacks you face. You may very well have prepared yourself for disappointment, and, if so, you need to dispense with those orders quickly.

"I keep the telephone of my mind open to peace, harmony, health, love, and abundance," wrote inspirational author Edith Armstrong. "Then, whenever doubt, anxiety, or fear try to call me, they keep getting a busy signal—and they'll soon forget my number."

That's a great metaphor for keeping your mind positive. But sometimes, just like cockroaches, fear and doubt do creep in through a crack that's so small you don't even realize it's there.

Napoleon Hill identified seven fears that strike everyone from time to time. These fears are most damaging when they limit your belief in what you can do. It's a small step then for them to begin limiting your action, which inevitably leads to disappointment.

The seven fears are explained next.

Fear of Poverty

This fear cuts two ways. Some people place all their faith in the simple accumulation of money. Nothing else is valuable to them, and so they have little value to anyone else. They won't do anything that doesn't guarantee a profit, so they stop taking risks and challenging themselves, and eventually stagnate. They often end up lonely.

Other people are so overwhelmed by this fear that they can never bring themselves to act in a way that will profit them. Money, they figure, will always be in short supply, so budgeting is a waste of time. Hard work will still leave them strapped for cash, they believe, so they don't bother to work much at all. They have no ambition because they don't even see the point of it. They usually stay poor.

If you suspect that this fear is holding you back, confront it. Develop affirmations and sparks that address this fear directly. Any time you hold back from doing something, challenge yourself. Ask whether you're afraid that success is impossible. And then start revving up your PMA and enthusiasm.

Fear of Criticism

People in thrall to this fear can be very difficult to spend time with. They often try to ward off a blow to their own ego by dispensing criticism of others freely. But the fear can manifest itself in other ways: Are you always eager to know what the newest trend is? Would you rather die than be seen in something that was fashionable last year?

> Positively revel in your love of what you want to become.

Fear of criticism can eat up tremendous amounts of goodwill and money. And, like fear of poverty, it can be a real hindrance to achieving your ambitions. Why take a risk if you fear humiliation when you fail? Why pursue your major purpose if other people think it's inappropriate or out of reach?

Why indeed?

The answer: because you truly do want something different.

To combat this fear, dwell on your statement of purpose. Positively revel in your love of what you want to become.

Any potential criticism will pale when your attention is focused on something you know is truly important.

Fear of Ill Health

This fear literally makes you sick. If you dwell on the possibility that you're not well, you'll begin to feel unwell, if for no other reason than because of nervous anxiety. And you may actually begin to manifest the symptoms you dread experiencing.

Fear of ill health can have its roots in an actual episode of sickness or just in fear of what sickness might bring. If you truly have been sick and can't shake the fear that illness will return, therapy might be in order. But I would also suggest that you focus your mind on the fact that you're well again. You beat your sickness.

If you're actually well, but you're bothered by every little ache, pain, or blemish, ask yourself when you were truly last sick. Keep a list of all the little pains you've had, and you'll soon find that none of them amounted to more than a muscle strain or a wart.

In either case, choose some affirmations that create and reinforce a feeling of sound health. Chip away at this fear, and its hold will loosen. You'll start to feel better, and your fear will have fewer opportunities to grip you.

Fear of Lost Love

This fear is similar to the fear of criticism but more sharply focused. We can fear criticism from anyone, but the circle of those whose love we can't stand to lose is much smaller. The root of this fear is a poor image of yourself.

Often, people who suffer this fear have concluded that there is some single quality that makes them unlovable. They fixate on their weight or their looks, their moneymaking ability, or their sense of humor. Then, they pour everything they have into that one quality. Nothing else is important to them but becoming thin, beautiful, rich, or funny.

And the bitter truth is, this is about the fastest way you make yourself unlovable. No one loves you for one thing alone. People love in 3-D; they don't love a one-dimensional creature who spends all of his or her time doing one thing.

If you think you might be limiting yourself this way, here's a way to combat it and strengthen your relationship at the same time: write a love letter. It doesn't have to be a romantic one; some people are constrained by fear of losing a parent's love or a child's love. But express your feelings openly, and then give or send it. You'll provoke a discussion that will enlighten you. Your loved one may not be as expressive as you are, but you'll see yourself in an entirely new way once you begin to get feedback.

Once you have a grip on the idea that this single quality isn't all that matters, you'll find a freedom and a new sense of possibility in your relationship.

Fear of Old Age

This fear isn't limited to people who remember the Eisenhower administration. It can grip anybody who thinks that somehow life has passed them by and they have no time left to make any real changes. You can succumb to it at twenty-five as easily as at seventy-five.

And once this fear has you, you simply stop growing. You figure that no rewards are possible, so effort no longer makes sense. The world seems full of people who are more active or more in tune, so you feel you can't compete with them. You just give up.

But think about this. A seventy-six-year-old woman had spent years doing fine embroidery work. At last, arthritis made holding the needle impossible, so she put down the needle and the hoop, and took up a paintbrush. Her name was Anna Mary Robertson Moses, but most people know her as Grandma Moses. Her work now hangs in museums throughout the United States and Europe.

Grandma Moses kept painting for the rest of her life—another twenty-five years of life that included at least twenty-five paintings after her one-hundredth birthday. Would she have seen all those glorious years if she had decided that life had passed her by when she stopped embroidering?

If Grandma Moses could embark on a career as a world-famous painter at seventy-six, you should be able to realize that you still have plenty of time left yourself.

Fear of Lost Liberty

Thankfully, here in America, there are few threats to our liberty, at least in comparison to the lives of people in authoritarian countries. We don't worry about secret police, pogroms, informers, or work camps. But this fear can still take root and manifest itself in worries that we're caught up in a never-ending cycle of work and drudgery, or that we're somehow part of a marginalized segment of society.

The result is usually anger and resentment. Any time something doesn't work out for us, we blame "the system," or our oppressors. If your answer to every disappointment is to blame your ethnicity or gender, for instance, you may be in the grips of this fear.

These factors can place obstacles in your way. But wake up and turn on the television! Look at what you see. The old barriers are crumbling. You may still encounter them, but the walls of oppression are full of holes. Instead of deciding that you're trapped, fight your way through and start pulling down the barricades from the other side!

And realize, too, that the person who is doing most to define you by a single characteristic is yourself.

Fear of Death

Nothing in this book will free you from the fact that we all die. We are of this world, and like all flesh, our days end. But fearing the inevitable is useless and paralyzing. There is no way to avoid death in the end, and if you let its inevitability control your life, you might as well surrender to it now.

Instead, make any peace that your religion or philosophy dictates, and then begin addressing life. For it's in life where you have control, in life where you're presently unhappy, and—for those who believe in an afterlife—in this life where you prepare yourself for the next. Surrender to the fear of death, and you make this life nothing but misery.

Enthusiasm is the antidote. A healthy hunger for something more, a passion for achieving it, a conviction that

tomorrow can be better than today—these are the elements of enthusiasm and the qualities that will allow you
to find the motivation to throw off the great fear.

You don't want to die, so don't act as if you will ten
minutes from now. Instead, act as if you're going to keep
on living forever. Reach out for new ideas, experiences,
and friendships. Strive for things you want to happen.
Take a risk: take action now.

Don't pass up the opportunity to become the person you want to be. Even the greatest blow doesn't
have to put limits on what you
can do. Aim high! Believe in what
you can accomplish, and test the
limits of that belief. Even if you
miss the highest mark, you'll still hit a loftier target than
if you aimed for something you were sure of reaching.

Applying your faith in yourself and your major purpose gives you definite proof of your progress and your
power. It makes the very world itself your ally. Don't pass
up the opportunity to become the person you want to be.

Act now and know that you will succeed.

Chapter 9

Dreaming Big and Small

"The imagination is the workshop of the soul wherein a man's destiny is fashioned."

—Napoleon Hill

This is a chapter about how to become imaginative.

Nonsense, you say. Imagination is something you're born with.

No, imagination is a skill, like driving a car or doing multiplication. You can learn it and use it all the time. And imagination will make it much, much easier for you to achieve your goals.

> Everyone who has ever been a success has been a dreamer of one sort or another.

People with imagination are often called dreamers, and that name isn't always complimentary. Dreamers are stigmatized as impractical, ineffective, and unrealistic, but this is another piece of incorrect, negative thinking that pervades our culture. In truth, dreamers can be powerful, world-changing people. Everyone who has ever been a success has been a dreamer of one sort or another.

Dreams, wonderful as they can be, need to be translated into reality. Whether your dreams go no further than your front door or they encompass the entire world, they will be unfulfilled unless you understand how to make them happen.

Two major issues are addressed in this chapter: first, how you can give your imagination room to flourish, and second, how you can turn the things you imagine into reality. Each step is liberating and exciting, and the only limits you'll encounter are the ones you impose on yourself.

CASTING OFF THE CHAINS

As children, we all have rich imaginary powers. We fill our lives with unseen playmates, and every story we hear seems to be about something happening to us. When Dorothy goes to meet the Wizard of Oz, we're right there with her. When Jack defeats the giant, we're there to cheer him on.

But in adolescence, we learn that imagination and reality are often powerfully at odds. School teaches us to solve problems according to formulas that have already been worked out. We're rewarded for fitting into patterns, particularly social ones. Complete high school. Go to college. Get a job. Get married. Have children.

These patterns aren't necessarily bad. They're intended to give us the skills and accomplishments we need to function in life. But they don't allow much room for individual variation. A young woman who has a child before she finishes high school, for instance, isn't going to find many people expecting her to go to college and embark on a career.

But why shouldn't she? The path she takes might not be much like the one followed by young women without a child, but she can still create a path that will make it possible to get a college degree and a good, interesting, fulfilling job. But creating that path will require imagination, which, unfortunately, is one quality that is discouraged, especially in people who have already deviated from the established patterns.

THE TWO-FOLD IMAGINATION

Napoleon Hill identified two ways that imagination works. *Synthetic imagination* takes existing ideas and applies them in a new way. *Creative imagination* brings forth something completely new.

While creative imagination seems more significant somehow, the two types are equally important. Ideas produced by synthetic imagination can often be applied more quickly because they arise out of procedures that people are already familiar with. When you try a different herb in a recipe, that's synthetic imagination. When a new version of a software program is released, it's the result of synthetic imagination. Creative imagination has the potential to be more revolutionary. But because it presents a fundamental change, it can either seem wonderful or confounding.

One way to make a creative idea more palatable and useful, to yourself and others, is to surround it with some synthetic ideas. New concepts may need a familiar context in order for people to evaluate them. Don't let pride

Without imagination, we'd all be living under trees, eating foraged food while stark naked.

in your creative abilities stand in the way of showcasing them in a situation where they can find application.

Imagination is to be encouraged. It's not dangerous, and it's not frivolous. Imagination is absolutely necessary for personal and social progress. Without imagination, we'd all be living under trees, eating foraged food while stark naked. Imagination created civilization, and imagination is needed for civilization to continue. So, please, set aside any ideas you have that imagination is a quality of thinking that you don't need. It doesn't matter whether life has been easy for you so far or you've had to struggle the whole way. You need imagination.

And you have imagination right now. Yes, I can prove it.

Try this exercise: Sit down in a quiet place. Set a timer for two minutes. Close your eyes. Now, for the next two minutes, you can think of anything you want to except shoes.

Go.

When your two minutes are up, I know you won't be successful. It's impossible not to think about something you're avoiding thinking about. Maybe you tried thinking about something utterly unrelated to shoes, say a symphony. But you were still conscious of the effort of not thinking about shoes, and they kept sneaking into your mind: sneakers, sandals, hiking boots, loafers, work boots, or slippers.

This little exercise in futility works (or is it fails?) because you have an imagination. It's powerful right now, but undisciplined. Your imagination operates all the time, but you tend to ignore it. You ignore your imagination because you're taught to ignore it, because it's working on something irrelevant or because it's working on something you don't want to think about. But the trick to having a useful imagination is not to ignore it, but to direct it.

Here's another exercise. Set yourself up as you did the last time in someplace where you won't be interrupted, and set the timer for two minutes. Now, think about nothing but shoes.

Go.

Of course, you probably weren't able to accomplish this either. Thinking about shoes reminds you of where you bought them, what you wore them for, what they cost, and whether you have an upcoming event to attend and need new ones. A whole string of other thoughts probably entered your mind, even if you wrenched it back to shoes again and again.

But this is a much more useful side of imagination. It finds connections. It recalls feelings and ideas. Imagination is associative and creative. It draws things together and then spins new things out. This is the side of imagination that you can tap into when you need it.

If you've been ignoring your imagination, you'll need to do some work before it becomes a powerful tool for you. You'll need to learn to guide your imagination and to value what you discover from it. You never know when your imagination can help you.

You'll need insight. You're going to need creative solutions to problems such as writing computer code, raising cash, or getting your kids more involved in their schoolwork. And, trust me, when that moment comes, you'll be glad you have a fertile imagination to back you up.

> **You must be able to direct and trust your imagination to profit from it.**

FLEXIBILITY TRAINING

You must be able to direct and trust your imagination to profit from it. Let's look at some exercises you can use to train your imagination to respond to your directions.

For any of these exercises, there are no right answers. The outcome isn't as important as the process of learning how to put your imagination to work. At this point, don't let yourself get hung up on details and practicality. You'll reach the point, fairly quickly, where you can effectively apply your imagination to overcome specific difficulties. But first, we'll work on the simple matter of giving your imagination direction.

You can't get there from here.

Most of us have a standard route we follow to and from work. Now plan five alternate routes to work, each one conforming to one of the sets of rules provided below. If you don't leave the house for work, choose another frequent destination, such as a grocery store or a school.

1. Plot a route in which you only make left turns.
2. Plot a route that crosses three different bodies of water.

3. Plot a route that you would take on horseback.
4. Plot a route on which you would see a hospital, a library, and a park.
5. Plot a route on which you don't see a gas station, a restaurant, or a car wash.

Obviously, there's no practical point to any of these routes, but plotting each of them engages your mind and imagination. You have to recall things you see every day or things that may be hard to find. You may discover that you have to go an awfully long way around to accomplish any of them. But the point here is to engage parts of your mind that you don't normally draw into when thinking about your commute. You're applying imagination to something you currently do automatically. You're becoming conscious of something that has become familiar and routine, tapping information you've stored but never applied.

Reinventing something you take for granted is one of the best ways you can apply imagination. If you feel blocked in your efforts or somehow can't resolve a problem with solutions that have worked before, you can adapt this exercise to find a new approach. It works even if you don't know exactly what kind of change you need to make. Choose some arbitrary factor, and work it into your question. For instance, ask yourself one of these questions: How would I solve this if there were no electricity? How would I solve this if I could only communicate by writing?

The key to this exercise is to begin examining a situation from the ground up. The specific wrinkle that you introduce into the equation isn't as important as what you discover when you begin rethinking everything. As always, keep notes about intriguing little ideas that occur as you ponder things. The solution you need may not appear in a single insight; you may still have to draw some connections between several new ideas.

Wonderful me

Write your name down the left-hand side of a piece of paper, one letter to a line. Now, for every letter of your name, write down something positive about yourself that begins with that letter. Here's an example:

N Nice
A Able
P Persuasive
O Open-minded
L Limitless
E Even-tempered
O Optimistic
N Neat

H Happy
I Imaginative
L Loving
L Lively

Your goal here is to stretch your mind to find a range of ideas. If your name happens to use the same letter several times (such as L, above), you may have to put some real thought into it. That's fine. In fact, you're better off because you're pushing yourself a little harder. There's a side benefit to this exercise of reminding yourself of some of your good qualities, but the real gain is in trying to work within a structure while being as creative as possible.

If your imagination leads you someplace useful or enlightening, don't be afraid to follow it.

You can change this exercise by using a word or words that represent the issue you're struggling to conquer. You can also write a sentence rather than a single word if that helps you express an idea better. With this approach, you're working to get in touch with ideas that you have and, perhaps, to discover some new ideas as well.

You may also discover that you keep coming back to some ideas that don't fit within the structure of the words. If that happens, write the idea down at the bottom of the page for later consideration. The formula of the word is only meant as a starting place: if your imagination leads you someplace useful or enlightening, don't be afraid to follow it.

Color my world

This exercise is adapted from a technique used to help people correct minor vision problems. Think of it also as a way to improve imaginary vision.

Choose a color, any color. Now, without getting up, try to think of everything in your home that is that color or has that color on it. It can be clothes or a painting, the cover of a book, or a dish in your kitchen. Write each thing down on a piece of paper. After five minutes, get up and start looking around. How many things did you miss? Are there things you thought were one color that weren't?

Now, choose another color and repeat the exercise. You probably won't get everything right this time either, but you'll do much better.

Even a few small pieces of information can prime your imaginative pump.

In this exercise, you rely largely on memory. The second time through, you have some clues and experience that allow you to draw connections you might have overlooked before. You'll remember certain kinds of items or places you'd forgotten (what is in that refrigerator?).

This is something else important to remember about imagination: it can be fed. When you don't have all you need to do a job, get input. Investigate. Even a few small pieces of information can prime your imaginative pump.

Contrary Thoughts

Imagination can help you overcome obstacles by circumventing them. Copy the statements below onto a piece of paper. Then write an opposing statement next to each of them.

1. I have insomnia.
2. I hate apples.
3. My feet hurt.
4. I watch too much television.
5. I'm too fat.

Now, look at each of the opposing statements you've written and think of a way to make it true. You may not want it to be true, but for the sake of the exercise, just do it.

The point here is to get your mind accustomed to thinking about alternative situations and ways to create them. Changing your bedtime may be an easy way to address the first item, but you could also take sleeping pills. Unhealthy for some, maybe, but an option, nonetheless. Don't dismiss options because they seem wrong at first. Maybe you really do need to make a huge change.

This exercise is easily adapted for all kinds of problem-solving. Just write down a description of something you don't like, then follow it with a statement of the opposite. Then try to find a way to make the opposite true.

All the exercises, in fact, are useful for directing your imagination to deal with something that is confounding you. They may not by themselves provide a solution, but they do focus your creative powers on an issue and let it set to work. Imaginations work at different speeds, so don't worry if you don't find a solution the first time you ponder a question. Feel free to repeat the directions from time to time, though, until your imagination begins to respond.

Also be aware that your imagination can continue whirring away in the background while you're focused on another task. If you don't find the solution you need after consciously applying yourself to the question, don't despair. Let your imagination work its magic. You may discover that the light of inspiration shines when you least expect it. You may see, hear, or read something and suddenly, eureka! You'll recognize a connection or solution that had previously eluded you.

You may not even realize you need a new approach to something. But, then, sitting there watching a baseball game,

But keep in mind that pondering an idea isn't the same as deciding to act on it.

for example, you'll feel a spark of an idea enter your mind. What would happen, you'll ask yourself, if we pack our product with a baseball cap with our logo on it? Wouldn't that help create a bond with the new users? If they wore it, would seeing the cap make their friends curious about our product? How many new orders could we get through this method? Or is there something better than a baseball cap that we could use?

The ideas that you'll glean from an engaged imagination can be profoundly helpful to you. You don't have to embrace every idea, but don't ever make the mistake of telling your imagination, "Enough!" Your rational faculties can sort out the implications of ideas. Leave your creative faculties free to pursue new things.

EMBRACING INSPIRATION

Once your imagination begins to provide you with ideas, you still need to consider whether those ideas are useful. Don't reject anything out of hand, unless it conflicts with your moral beliefs. But keep in mind that pondering an idea isn't the same as deciding to act on it. There's nothing wrong—and perhaps a great deal right—with thinking something over and then abandoning it.

But the time will come when you must leap after looking. No matter how bountiful your imagination has become, it won't be much help to you unless you start to
act on the ideas it comes up with. The need to act on
your ideas is what makes imagination similar to faith.
You must begin to apply your imagination and to take
concrete steps to fulfill it. Unless you give your imagination expression, you'll be sending it a signal that it's not
important. You may find that your imagination becomes
less active or turns once again to subjects that aren't useful to you.

Some of us are much more comfortable with change
than others. If you're the kind of person for whom change
brings anxiety or resistance, you can still embrace imagination. The key for you, and for all of us, really, is to make
embracing imagination familiar. As with applying faith,
you can begin with small steps that demonstrate to yourself that change can be welcome.

Remember the first imagination exercise presented in
this chapter of changing your route to work? Why not try
a change as small and as simple as that? You don't need
to do anything as drastic as riding to work on a horse,
though. Tomorrow, when you leave the house, turn left
if you normally turn right, or vice versa. Then follow the
shortest route you know (short of turning right back
around).

This small change may seem inconsequential, but make
it with your eyes open. Ask yourself if there are any benefits. Do you pass a place that you need to stop at anyway?
Do you avoid a crowded intersection or a dangerous

stretch of road? It may be that this little change completely alters your entire commute, or it could take you back to your familiar route very quickly. And this is something worth realizing about changes. They can be profound or unimportant, but when you make them consciously, you're prepared for them, if only in the sense that you remain able to make adjustments.

There are other ways you can accustom yourself to change. Alter the way you answer the phone. Get up an hour earlier. Eat vegetarian for a week. (Whatever it is, choose something where you're not likely to upset someone else by adopting the new approach. You don't want to have someone

Keep making little changes until you no longer resist the concept of change.

complaining while you're trying something new. You want to concentrate on your own reactions, not someone else's.) Keep making little changes until you no longer resist the concept of change. You'll start to discover that some of the changes are worth incorporating into your daily routine because there isn't a person out there who has discovered the perfect way of doing everything in his or her life.

Change will begin to seem like an ally. You'll have a dawning sense that even if everything doesn't work out every time, change is still useful and exciting. You'll also gain some confidence in your ability to predict the results of new ideas. You'll see you were right that drinking your coffee black meant you drank less and became less dependent on it. You'll see you were right to suspect that eating lunch at your desk didn't save you time because you kept answering the phone. You'll decide that the reading time you gained by taking the bus to work wasn't worth the extra time it took, but that getting up earlier cut fifteen minutes off your drive time.

Small realizations lead to larger ones. Your willingness to make changes, as well as your ability to adjust to and evaluate them, will increase steadily. Now you've prepared yourself for something larger.

This can be a big step. The solutions that imagination produces often touch on the unknown or untried. This newness is an important part of their value, but it still requires a risk on your part. You can prepare yourself in several ways for taking an imaginative leap.

Talk about it with your Master Mind group. You may discover knowledge and perspectives that are very valuable (that's what the Master Mind is there to provide). This new information can help you refine your idea and may even drastically increase its usefulness.

Time things carefully. Make sure you have the resources—time, money, personnel, emotional energy—to adjust to a change and, if necessary, to its complications. A good idea may alter things you do not anticipate, and if you panic at the first ripple in the pond, you won't be able to evaluate whether your change is worthwhile.

Think everything through first. Again, draw your Master Mind group into this. There may be some costs involved, so decide whether you're willing to bear them in exchange for the benefits you'll receive. Make a list of all the good results you expect, and make another list next to it of any possible drawbacks. Consider ways to eliminate the drawbacks while deriving the benefits you want. There will still be no guarantee of success, but you'll have eliminated foreseeable stumbling blocks.

Make the change with PMA. As with anything you do, going in with an optimistic attitude makes an enormous difference. Your expectations color your actions, as well as the actions of anyone else involved. If a coworker or a client senses that you're nervous, that anxiety will be communicated. If they sense you're enthusiastic, well, you know what you'll sense in them as well.

Evaluate as you go. You're making a change to achieve a result. Changes are not made for the sake of change but for improvement. You can and must ask yourself hard questions about whether you're truly benefiting from this new way. Don't ask the question the moment you encounter your first complication, though. Enact a solution, and then, when you have a quiet minute, consider whether this first sign of trouble is going to recur and if there is a way to address it.

You may have to decide that no matter how brilliant your idea seemed, it simply isn't workable. If you choose to abandon it, apply the lessons on learning from defeat to gain an understanding of why you didn't realize the benefits you wanted. Don't berate yourself for a failed idea. Even Leonardo da Vinci's notebooks are full of schemes that he was never able to make work.

Don't stifle your imagination because it led to a disappointment. The mark of true inspiration is a willingness to keep on imagining even in the face of failure. When

Clare Boothe Luce was booed off a Broadway stage, she didn't decide that she would never write another play. And her willingness to keep imagining what she could do eventually brought her to a seat in Congress and made her the American ambassador to Italy.

Your imagination can transform you. That transformation will only take place, however, if you're willing to translate your visions into something real. Dream all you want, but don't stop with the dream. Work. Act. Make mistakes. Examine those mistakes. Try again. Dreams are only a beginning. You must trust your dreams to realize them, and you must put that trust into action.

Chapter 10

Putting the World on a String

"A pleasing personality is a well-rounded one; accordingly, there are twenty-five different aspects of your personality you must strive to improve. Some of them are a positive mental attitude, flexibility, habit of smiling, tolerance, and a sense of justice."

—Napoleon Hill

Fire up that imagination of yours and envision this: everywhere you go, you meet people who respond to you with enthusiasm. They listen to what you have to say, and they want to hear more. These people are eager to help you: they want to buy what you're selling, to support your efforts to change the world. People are drawn to you. They admire you, and many of them try to emulate you. You've discovered how to present yourself in a way that inspires trust, confidence, and respect. You have what Napoleon Hill called a *pleasing personality*.

Creating a pleasing personality does wonders for your efforts to achieve your major purpose. It engenders cooperation and goodwill, opens doors, and instills friendly attitudes in other people. You capture the interest of everyone, and you can use that interest to gain great advantages.

If you've been applying lessons from the previous chapters, you'll already have qualities that go into a pleasing personality: positive attitude, enthusiasm, a sense of purpose, the ability to deal with setbacks, self-discipline, and creativity. When you make a conscious effort to display these qualities to other people, you acquire all the fundamentals of being an attractive person. What remains is discovering the means to showcase these aspects of yourself so that they draw people to you.

As with so many things you're doing to achieve your goals, you accomplish this through steady effort that begins with seemingly small things. The suggestions that follow in this chapter may sometimes strike you as simplistic and unimportant, but they're not. When you consider each one and realize how that quality affects you when another person displays it, you'll understand how useful it can be.

Presenting an appealing personality isn't a matter of inhibiting yourself so that you seem just like everyone around you. Your own special qualities will still have room for expression. Indeed, they will probably be highlighted by your efforts. You'll understand your strengths and be able to play to them. You don't have to worry about becoming a cookie-cutter image of a perfect person. You'll remain yourself, and others will see that unique self more clearly than ever before.

Let's examine all the things that go into a pleasing personality. Some of them loom larger than others, but each one is worth considering in terms of how you display it to everyone you meet. There are many aspects to a pleasing personality. Don't let that daunt you, though. As you'll discover, many of these elements are qualities you've already been working on.

POSITIVE MENTAL ATTITUDE

When I introduced you to the idea of Positive Mental Attitude many pages ago, I asked you to consider whom you'd rather spend time with, someone upbeat and vigorous, or someone depressing and boring. I'll assume your answer is still the same.

PMA is optimistic as well as realistic, and both of these qualities need to seem evident to other people. Confidence and a can-do attitude are attractive on their own, but if your sunny nature never seems to acknowledge problems at all, then people are going to begin to mistrust your judgment. Don't fall into the trap of thinking that PMA means you can't admit that there are problems to solve. Acknowledge issues, and then demonstrate that you're sure you'll find an answer for them.

When you find the answer, presenting your solution in an affirmative manner will rally people to your idea. Work a little enthusiasm into your presentation as well, and be ready to act with some applied faith. Take a leading role, especially in situations where leadership seems to be absent, and you'll inspire other people to follow.

If you reinforce your PMA every day, before you go out into the world, you'll emerge with an energy that will attract people wherever you go. A smile and a friendly greeting have an infectious quality: spread some PMA around at work early in the morning, and it will influence your encounters with others throughout the day. Say your goodbyes in the same manner. Send other people home with a good feeling about you, their work, and themselves. If they carry some of your PMA home, it can affect their entire evenings and bring them back to work the next day even more receptive to you.

> **By creating an affinity with people, you encourage them to see your needs and goals as akin to theirs.**

Even if the PMA you share doesn't last until you next meet someone, they will still associate you with their own sense of greater energy and potential. That bond works wonders when you need help or assistance. By creating an affinity with people, you encourage them to see your needs and goals as akin to theirs. Make yourself memorable through PMA, and you'll find plenty of new allies in your quest for success.

FLEXIBILITY

In the middle of a presentation to senior management, a corrupted file snarls your visuals, and a picture appears on the screen of your family on vacation. It's cute, but

hardly to the point. You can't correct the problem immediately. Do you:

a) blame your assistant?
b) give up?
c) continue the presentation?

The answer, of course, is C.

Keeping yourself focused and able to cope with frustra-
tions is an essential part of having a pleasing personality.
PMA helps with this, as does the emotional understanding that comes with self-discipline. If you recognize your
feelings, you're better able to keep them in check and do
what it takes to manage them. You're also able to sense
and adjust to changes in the emotional states of others. Keeping your mood in line with the atmosphere in
a given situation is important, unless you want to seem
completely out of touch.

If a time comes when you sense that a mood needs to
change, being emotionally flexible means that you're able to
project a countering feeling. You can inject optimism where
it's needed, or break up tension when people are at logger-
heads. You can shift a group reaction to a piece of news,
from anxiety to a sense of opportunity. In a negotiation,
you're able to understand what is important to the other
party; this makes you able to offer them what they need.

Emotional flexibility isn't the same as emotional im-
pressionability. You must analyze and evaluate the moods
you encounter in others before you make a response.

Doing this allows you to diffuse antagonism with understanding, or turn a complication into chance to make
things better.

People who are emotionally flexible are seen as problem solvers. They
have reputations for not being overwhelmed by circumstances. They
become essential parts of organi-
zations and are trusted to make decisions on their own.
Keep yourself flexible and become one of these people.

> **People who are emotionally flexible are seen as problem solvers.**

SINCERITY

This is the touchstone of a pleasing personality. All the
acting talent in the world won't give you a pleasing personality without a sincere belief in yourself and the importance of your purpose in life. When you're acting from
conviction, from a deeply seated, passionately held belief,
the intensity of your feelings is conveyed to other people.
Attempt to use the other attributes of a pleasing personality for the wrong ends, and your lack of sincerity will
sabotage you.

Sincerity requires a good deal of self-examination and
understanding. If you suspect that your major purpose
is somehow unworthy, you'll betray that feeling. If you
attempt to enlist the aid of someone you don't believe
shares some common ground with you, you'll lack the
sincerity to win that person over. You must convince
yourself before anyone else of the importance of your
purpose in life.

This is not to say that you have to know that another person believes exactly as you do. But you must find a point of connection, an idea, or an issue where your be-liefs are similar. And it's from this nexus that you can begin to make your appeal for friendship and re-spect. You can display sincerity with the clerk at the motor vehicles office who is renewing your driver's li-cense, with a doctor who's treating you for the flu, or with someone who's vitally important to achieving your goals. Each of these people has a role to play in helping you succeed. The size of the role varies, but any one of them will be friendlier and more helpful when they perceive that you sincerely understand and re-spect what they can do for you.

Sincerity can balloon into overzealousness if you don't have a rein on your enthusiasm.

You can project greater sincerity by making sure that you're convinced of the importance of your major pur-pose. Read your statement of purpose every day, and do it with some passion and feeling. Keep your enthusiasm active and under control: you want to display it when nec-essary, but you don't want to overwhelm people with it. Sincerity can balloon into overzealousness if you don't have a rein on your enthusiasm.

Sincerity will also allow you to make difficult points with people. If they understand that you're not simply seeking a temporary advantage, they'll listen to you more closely. You'll be able to inspire them more effectively, and get them to consider choices they might not make on their own. This is just as true for a parent talking to a teenager as it is for a manager trying to rally employees to work harder.

Sincerity is infectious. Your belief in the importance of your purpose can inspire people to work harder for you, with greater inspiration. Show sincerity in all your dealings, and you'll be emboldened by what you can accomplish.

> **Show sincerity in all your dealings, and you'll be emboldened by what you can accomplish.**

FIRMNESS

Hand in hand with sincerity comes firmness. Most often, this is displayed in decision-making, but it's also important in the opinions you voice. Firmness isn't the same as rigidity. A rigid personality simply sticks to an idea because it can't accept a new one. A firm personality backs choices with solid reasons and becomes something that people can depend on.

You'll find it easy to be firm when you've got strong self-discipline. Making a decision and then changing your mind is a sign of conflicting emotions. It's fine to initially be ambivalent about something, but once you decide to act, you have to realize that other people depend on what you've decided to do. That's why it's important to be disciplined in your thinking and not to make choices based on a whim.

The principle also applies when you offer an opinion. If you need time to think something through, take it. But once you open your mouth, don't pepper your speech with qualifications. You'll give people the impression that you're unsure or indecisive.

Having a strong identification with your major purpose makes it much easier to be firm. You can make your choice based on what's most important to you. If that requires a sacrifice, you'll know why you're making it. You can avoid tempting distractions, and can choose paths that take you toward your goal.

> **Having a strong identification with your major purpose makes it much easier to be firm.**

And if the time comes when you must admit a mistake, do it. Don't offer an equivocal admission. A firm declaration that someone else was correct will win you much more respect than a qualified admission. People will trust your firm declarations more when they don't suspect that you're incapable of acknowledging an error when it happens.

COURTESY

Oh, there are so many examples I could give you of how courtesy has disappeared from the world. By courtesy, I mean people who treat each other with respect. Display some courtesy to people, and you'll instantly rise a few notches in their estimation.

Courtesy isn't old-fashioned stuffiness. It's showing sensitivity for other people's feelings under all circumstances, even people you encounter for only a few seconds. It's helping people and being kind to them.

Courtesy is rare enough these days that you'll make an instant impression.

Here are some ways to display common courtesy:

- Hold a door open long enough for the person behind you to be able to hold it themselves. Letting a door slam behind you in someone else's face is a fast way of saying you don't care about that person.
- Make eye contact with people when you speak to them. People who have to deal with you while you shuffle papers or talk on the phone get the impression that you're annoyed with or not interested in them.
- When you're calling someone you've never met, address them by Ms. or Mr. and their last name. How often do you get a call for you by your first name, only to discover it's a telephone solicitation? Don't bother yourself with intruders like this.
- Don't be afraid to remind someone you barely know of your own name. This prevents awkwardness and puts them at ease. It also provides a compliment to them if they do remember your name.
- Don't let cell phone calls interrupt face-to-face conversations. If you have to answer the call, tell the caller you'll get back to them. Nobody likes waiting while you show them that someone else is more important.
- Don't insert yourself into the middle of another conversation to ask questions that are totally unrelated. You force the other people to get off topic, and you suggest that they aren't as important as you are.

These examples are really here just to remind you of ways to be conscious of how you're treating other people. If you make courtesies a habitual part of your behavior, you'll be ensuring that you never inadvertently insult your next big client or new neighbor. Even the people you're not dealing with most directly or frequently will learn that you're aware of them as human beings deserving of respect. These small gestures of respect can weigh very heavily.

TACT

Tactfulness isn't the same thing as courtesy. Tact is more self-serving than courtesy. Where courtesy shows

> **Being tactful requires sensitivity and thinking before you speak or act.**

respect, tact is a means of keeping your foot and ankle out of your mouth. When you have tact, you avoid giving people the impression that you're a runaway train who can't be trusted to show good judgment.

You can be courteous and untactful at the same time. Offer a seat to someone who doesn't seem as able as you are to stand, and you're being courteous. Say, "You look like you're about to fall over. Take my seat," and you undo all the good of being courteous.

Being tactful requires sensitivity and thinking before you speak or act. Few people want to appear tactless, but here are some common errors that we all sometimes make:

- Asking personal questions that are none of your business
- Assuming other people share your religious or political beliefs
- Giving your opinion unsolicited
- Gossiping
- Correcting other people's errors in front of a third party

Being tactful isn't the same as being timid. If you need to inject a contrary opinion into a discussion, try asking a question rather than making a challenge. If you need to ask a question that may cause embarrassment to someone, choose a time when other people won't overhear. Tact isn't an excuse to avoid issues. But if you raise a tender subject in an appropriate way, you'll find that you end up discussing the problem rather than dealing with an angry reaction to your insensitivity.

That's the real purpose of tact in a pleasing personality: you put the focus of an interaction on what's truly important. Be tactful, and you'll accomplish more and leave an impression of yourself as someone who is discerning and trustworthy.

FRANKNESS

It may seem odd to follow tact with frankness. Most people think they are opposites. But tact is more a matter of timing, and frankness is a matter of honesty. It's not tactful to lie to someone, nor is it tactful to speak so vaguely that no one knows what you mean.

Frankness isn't an excuse to be rude. You can be direct without being insulting. If someone asks your opinion, and you have an honest objection, make it. But choose your words carefully so that you convey your meaning clearly without picking a fight. Better to say, "I'm concerned about what will happen when . . ." than "This will be a disaster."

Be aware that frankness extends to the questions you ask other people. Don't go fishing for compliments to trap someone into saying something nice. Don't ask questions when you don't want to hear an honest answer. This is plain old manipulation.

Keeping your emotions in check with self-discipline makes

> **Frankness isn't an excuse to be rude.**

frankness possible. You can express disagreement without causing a confrontation. You can also be confident that your ideas are based on sound reasoning and not some issue you don't want to acknowledge.

Frank people are valued for their opinions. People feel they can trust you, especially when your frankness extends to offering compliments. When others know where they stand with you, they'll be more willing to extend themselves to work with you or help you.

VOICE

Almost no one likes the sound of their own voice when they hear a recording of it. It never sounds the same as you thought it did. However, you've probably noticed that the world isn't full of people with ugly voices. As disturbing as a recording of your voice can be, you most likely don't have an unpleasant voice.

What you should strive to become conscious of is the tone of your voice in different situations. Most of us get louder when talking about something that excites us. But you don't want a tone or volume of voice that's intrusive. Instead, work for an even, confident tone, and make sure that the stresses in your sentences occur when and where you want them.

Record yourself saying the following: I want the job done tomorrow.

This is a sentence that can easily come across in a belligerent tone. But it's exactly the kind of idea you need to express often without sounding strident, angry, or excited. Try placing the stress on different words in the sentence, then listen to the recording to see how it sounds to your own ears. Consider how you'd respond to a request given to you in the various tones. Place a stress with a rising tone on "done." You'll sound more confident and less dictatorial than if you stress "I" or "want" or "tomorrow." A falling tone on a stressed word will sound ominous and threatening.

Most of the time, you probably won't have to be so direct in your conversation. But it's still important to become aware of how you're getting your points across. People whose voices sound reasonable and poised project that image of themselves. If your voice tends to get higher when you're talking about something important, you'll give others the impression that your emotions are running away from you. You can inspire confidence as long as you control the pitch and the volume at all times.

LANGUAGE

Different professions and lives require different vocabu-
laries. Whatever your major purpose, you want to be certain that the words you use are appropriate and that they
have the desired effect on the people you're talking to.

If you're not confident about your vocabulary, do some
reading with a dictionary nearby. The daily newspaper is
a great choice for most people. The words it uses won't be
so uncommon that you'll confuse people, but you won't
be picking up slang either. If your calling involves a specialized vocabulary, read all that you can to develop your
knowledge of that vocabulary. Don't use words to impress people with your intelligence. Use words that make
sense in your conversation. Never insert a word into your
speech when you're not completely sure of its meaning.

Precise speech conveys a precise meaning. This is the fastest possible way to
make yourself sound ignorant.

Become aware of commonly mis-
understood words and words that
aren't standard English. Read Strunk and White's *The Elements of Style* for some pointers in this area. You can get
away with nonstandard words in many situations, but it's
better to excise them from your usage so they don't slip in
when you don't want them.

The purpose of building a good vocabulary is to make
sure you're communicating what you want to communicate. This occurs on two fronts. Precise speech conveys a
precise meaning. You'll always benefit from that. But your
vocabulary also sends a message about you. The more you

understand this, the better you'll be able to suit what you're saying to your listeners. In the same hour, you may need to display technical expertise to one person and then you may need to reassure someone else that you're approachable and able to speak in everyday language. If you use the same words for each person, you'll run the risk of alienating at least one of them.

Your word choices tell others that they can talk to you. Well-chosen language makes you accessible and respected. You don't have to sound like an English professor (unless you are one), but when your speech is clear and easily understood, you'll find that you make people willing to talk with you. From this small beginning, you can build the kind of relationships you need.

> A small, friendly smile is an effective way of establishing a connection to people.

SMILE

A smile isn't a cure-all for every difficult situation. However, a small, friendly smile is an effective way of establishing a connection with people. It's much better to begin an encounter with a smile than to adopt one nervously when you decide things aren't going your way.

The world is full of people who act as if smiling would kill them. Their lack of a smile carries over into their whole attitude toward dealing with others. If you greet people with a smile, you instantly separate yourself from these miserable people. Occasionally, you may even find that you shock one of them into smiling back. At the very least, you're sending a message that you're not beginning

Putting on a friendlier face can be very helpful at the right time, especially when you're asking for help.

your engagement in a confrontational mode. And, of course, smiling affects you: it often triggers your enthusiasm and promotes the extension of courtesies.

Don't keep a smile on your face when it's clearly inappropriate. You'll just look silly. It never hurts to check yourself mid-conversation to see if you're indeed smiling. Putting on a friendlier face can be very helpful at the right time, especially when you're asking for help.

OTHER FACIAL EXPRESSIONS

While a smile is often useful, it isn't always appropriate. There are times when you need to show interest or even convey disagreement in situations where a smile would send the wrong message. Other expressions can also be inappropriate: you certainly don't want your face to betray boredom or distaste to people without your knowing it.

Your eyes and your mouth are the two places where your face most often shows your reactions. As you talk to people, make sure that you aren't narrowing your eyes or pursing your lips unconsciously. These expressions can creep up on you if you're not paying attention to them. Even small contractions can affect the way you look, so it might help to experiment in front of a mirror.

Become sensitive to the feelings of the muscles in your face, so that you can recognize and correct a look that isn't useful.

One safe place to practice being conscious of your expression is on the phone because you don't actually have a viewing audience. If you have to, in these situations, you can smile like a loon to train yourself not to frown or squint as you speak. You'll also discover that the expression you choose has an effect on your voice and mood. Just as acting enthusiastically brings on feelings of enthusiasm, trying to look interested or confident will infuse your voice and attitude with these same qualities.

You're not trying to trick people. You're trying to focus on and convey the aspects of your own feelings that are most helpful to your efforts. While it's entirely possible that you feel nervous or tense in the course of a conversation, if the person you're talking with sees only enthusiasm and interest, you'll make a much stronger impression.

HUMOR

A robust sense of humor cuts through many tense situations and creates bonds quickly. Your sense of humor doesn't have to be comedian class, and you don't need a huge repertoire of jokes. Often, all it may take is the willingness to laugh, at yourself as much as the situation you're in, to put people at ease with you.

Some fairly obvious points: don't make jokes at other people's expense. If your effort at humor fails, don't force the issue. Move on. Don't let a little storytelling become a long diversion from the matter at hand. And when you make a joke at your own expense, don't reinforce a negative idea about yourself. It's much better to exaggerate a good quality in a jocular way than to play the buffoon. If you make a joke about your own mistake, move on quickly to the correction: you'll still have created some goodwill, and other people will focus on your honesty and quick thinking, not on your mistake.

Developing a healthy sense of humor goes hand in hand with being flexible. It shows you aren't paralyzed by bad news and that disappointment and anger aren't dominant in your makeup. It will also make other people more willing to come to you with news of their own problems, and you'll be able to start working on solutions that much sooner.

A GOOD HANDSHAKE

A handshake is often the only physical contact you have with people. It can give them a unique impression of you. You want to project strength and confidence without suggesting that you're overbearing. You don't need a workout routine to have a good handshake. It's a very simple action, and all it requires is that you grasp the other person's hand fully, so that your palms are touching. Grip the hand once, firmly, but without engaging in a wrestling match. Hold for just a moment, then withdraw.

Shaking hands with someone whose hand feels limp is unsettling. It's like grabbing a dead fish. You don't want that image in people's minds. Similarly, just offering your fingers instead of your whole hand suggests reticence or weakness. But don't try to force the other person to their knees with your vice-like handshake, either, because you'll make them instantly offended or intimidated.

A handshake can seem like an old-fashioned skill, but there's a visceral connection made when two people touch. When you determine the nature of that connection, you're presenting yourself in a way that presents the image of yourself that you want. Don't overlook this small gesture as an important factor in the impression you make.

FAIRNESS

In your Master Mind arrangement, you understand that work and rewards have to be distributed fairly. You need to adopt this same attitude in all your dealings with other people. Being known as a fair dealer makes people confident in you, and it gives you a rock-solid sense of personal integrity. When you have to make difficult choices, other people—and you—will know that your decision is based on what's right, not necessarily on what benefits you.

Create a reputation for being fair, and you'll find that more people are willing to work with you. They'll understand that you aren't going to use their cooperation against them. Building bridges in this way allows you to accomplish things that selfish people can't. Yes, there may be a few people who try to exploit your fairness, but when you call them out on it, they won't be able to point out any similar actions by you.

Fairness goes hand in hand with honesty, but it also requires judgment. You might have to cut someone some slack, and you also need to know when to draw a line. With strong self-discipline, it's easier to make these kinds of calls. You can analyze your feelings and see if and how they're affecting your opinions. In work situations, as well as in family settings and in friendships, there are plenty of emotional reasons to support one person or idea over another. These reasons may or may not have anything to do with what's appropriate from a fairness perspective. You must distinguish between the two possibilities before you make your call. If you're known as someone who doesn't play favorites, you won't find yourself accused of partisanship.

> There is no substitute for the kind of respect you earn when you act justly.

Fairness is particularly important for people in leadership positions. When your subordinates know that you'll give them an honest hearing and that your decisions will be based on a sincere desire to do what is right, you'll become a more inspiring figure. There is no substitute for the kind of respect you earn when you act justly.

PIZZAZZ

Pizzazz is what Napoleon Hill called "showmanship." It's the ability to know when and how to call attention to yourself and your ideas. Both *when* and *how* are important.

If you're always demanding attention from other people, you won't get it without going to greater and greater extremes. Ultimately, this won't work, just like a child whose parents stop responding to tantrums. If, on the other hand, you know the right time to turn the spotlight on yourself, you'll find that other people follow your lead. Don't try to be the star when it's someone else's turn to shine. Wait and select your moment carefully so that you can get the kind of attention you need when you need it. Attention isn't useful by itself: it has to be drawn when something important is happening.

How you draw the attention is up to you. It can be a simple matter of language or the tone of voice you use. You can change

Self-confidence allows you to display pizzazz.

your appearance, write a memo, or even do a little dance. What matters is that the method you use is appropriate to the situation. If you're at a long meeting where people are being bombarded with information, you can try something funny or dramatic. The change will be welcomed. If you're brainstorming a solution to an emergency, don't call attention to yourself: focus it on your idea. That's what people need right then.

Self-confidence allows you to display pizzazz. You have to be willing to put yourself out there and get attention. Revving up your enthusiasm also helps. Don't force yourself to do anything unnatural; you'll just call attention to your awkwardness. But don't hesitate to speak up strongly when the moment comes. Pizzazz is a very personal quality. Yours doesn't have to be like anyone else's. It only needs to work for you when you decide to employ it.

HUMILITY

This is the opposite of pizzazz. It doesn't mean hiding yourself in the washroom when the company is handing out service awards, though. It means eliminating arrogance and vanity from your behavior. Strange as it may seem, humility requires self-confidence just as pizzazz does: you must be able to let your accomplishments speak for themselves.

> **You must be able to let your accomplishments speak for themselves.**

If someone compliments you, the humble response is to thank them sincerely. The importance of a compliment lies in the recognition that is bestowed on you. If you brush the compliment away, you're not showing respect for the person who gave it to you. If you take the compliment as an invitation to list all your other accomplishments, you're implying that the other person didn't really know enough to offer the compliment.

Humility isn't timidity. Mother Teresa was a very humble person, but that didn't keep her from walking through the streets of Calcutta to help the poor. It didn't keep her from conversing with Popes and prime ministers, and even challenging them to do more to help the poor. Part of humility lies in understanding that what is important to you isn't necessarily important to others. When Mother Teresa asked for help in doing her work, she didn't make the appeal personal. She didn't say, "I need help." As beloved a figure as she was, she made her appeals in the name of the poor. She kept the focus where it needed to be.

And humility doesn't come from talking yourself down. There will be times when you absolutely must talk yourself up! But you can still do this humbly by concentrating on accomplishments and goals, not on what those things say about you. A humble person displays perspective and sound judgment. This person wins respect and cooperation by recognizing that he or she has something to prove, and then proving it through actions, not words.

FAITH

Applied faith is a very beguiling characteristic. When you show that you can act in an optimistic manner and make things happen, you remind everyone that this same choice is available to them. People will want to work with you, to share in your productivity and your good spirits.

Seeing beliefs made into something concrete is inspiring and uplifting.

Applied faith is at the root of a pleasing personality for this very reason. People are drawn to someone who reminds them of the best aspects of themselves. You're putting into action what most people only dream about for themselves. Seeing beliefs made into something concrete is inspiring and uplifting.

All the most important elements of a pleasing personality are manifested in applied faith: PMA, flexibility, sincerity, honesty, and humility. Applied faith is the outward manifestation of what you believe in. It's your personality translating itself into deeds—important deeds. You can't completely ignore the other elements of a pleasing personality in favor of applied faith, but when you've made it your dominating mode of action, many of these elements will start to fall in line.

The way you present yourself to the world is wholly within your control. There may be things about your appearance that you can't change; you may have to work around ideas that other people have about you based on gender, race, age, or physical ability. But you can still show anyone that you're a positive, thoughtful person of action. In that demonstration, you'll gain influence and respect, cooperation, and opportunity.

Some of the qualities mentioned in this chapter may seem less important than others, but every one of them provides you with the means for displaying important parts of yourself. As you work on one, you'll find that it necessarily draws in a few other elements, which is all to the good. A personality isn't a string of individual qualities: it's an integrated whole, the sum of traits that add up to something unique. Even once you've adopted all the elements set forth here, you'll still remain uniquely *you* because at the core of your actions lies your definite major purpose.

Whatever it is, that goal that you're after, you're well on your way now to understanding how you can make it happen. That awareness alone should convince you to draw on every tool you can. Your personality is just such a tool. It's also a reflection of how you're growing and becoming stronger as you learn. Let the lessons you read here become a part of you, and you'll reach your goals fully convinced that it was you, not luck, that made it happen.

Chapter 11

Living a Value-Added Life

"A man is great only when he makes his part of the world better."

—Napoleon Hill

Going the extra mile means doing more than is expected and giving better service than called for by the circumstances. It's an attitude toward your relationships with other people that must become a habit before you can reach your goals. This approach will cost you time, effort, and maybe even money in the short term, but in the long term, it prepares you for great things. When it becomes a part of your thinking, when it's your constant state of mind, you'll have made yourself ready to excel.

Just exactly how you go the extra mile depends on your abilities, your situation, and your goals. You can work without pay. Or you can do more work than you're paid for. You can work harder than your job requires, with a better attitude than anyone expects. You can provide a free service to your clients or customers. You can work to improve your skills without being paid to, and then use those skills without expecting a raise.

What's important is that you do this something extra without expecting to be rewarded for it. Going the extra mile isn't an excuse to ask for a raise or any other kind of advantage. It has to be something you offer freely, solely for the sake of doing a better job.

In an era when people jealously guard their rights and privileges, it may seem strange to think about offering more of yourself than you're expected to. The prevailing philosophy says that we should all be looking to get the maximum return on our investment, be it time, money, or effort: doing anything else is irresponsible and, well, foolish. Why give freely something that you could be investing profitably in something else?

Well, you are investing it. It's just that the return you're going to see doesn't show up on a balance statement or a paycheck immediately. But it won't take long for you to understand how you're benefiting.

THE LAW OF INCREASING RETURNS

Despite its name, this isn't a principle that your broker will discuss with you. The Law of Increasing Returns is a phenomenon by which the quantity and quality of your extra service comes back to you greatly multiplied. In other words, one good turn deserves ten others. Or twenty. Or a hundred.

This may sound fanciful and unrealistic, but the concept is quite real. Say you plant an apple seed. It takes some time for the apple tree to grow, but once it's just a few years old, it starts to bear fruit. The very first apple off that tree has ten times the number of seeds that you planted, and you'll have more apples every year for decades, each one full of seeds.

The service and work you do by going the extra mile aren't multiplied quite as predictably. The quantity and timing of rewards are always idiosyncratic, but the rewards do come. The key to benefiting from the Law of Increasing Returns is your attitude. If you're grudging about the work you do or always looking for an immediate payback, you'll poison your chances of getting rewards. You have to offer extra work and service happily, willingly, and without an eye on your wallet. Think of it this way: you're not earning anything by going the extra mile, you're preparing yourself to receive something.

You prepare yourself by learning to work hard, by keeping your mental attitude positive, and by being alert for the chance to do something better. When going the extra mile is a habit for you, you train yourself to always ask, how could this be done better? That attitude—whether you're a surgeon or seamstress—constantly forces you to improve yourself. You strengthen your skills, you challenge accepted ways of doing things, and you become better at your work than ever before. Just as an athlete conditions himself to win, you condition yourself to succeed. Small daily training leads to victory.

And it's then that another law comes into play.

THE LAW OF COMPENSATION

The Law of Compensation holds that everything you do brings you a result of a similar kind. This idea is at the heart of Napoleon Hill's ideas. You'll gain nothing worthwhile without giving something worthwhile in return. If you try to cheat your way to success, eventually, this law will catch up with you, and you'll lose your ill-gotten gains faster than you stole it.

But if you steadily offer something extra, something beyond the call of duty, you're also going to be rewarded with things outside the familiar pattern of remuneration. This reward doesn't always appear immediately, but it does inevitably come your way.

Once again, your attitude is important. Don't go the extra mile expecting someone to walk up to you and say, "Gee, you've really put some effort into this. Here's a bonus." People can sense this expectation on your part, and they'll resent it. It's like being a doorman with your hand always twitching at your side, waiting for a tip. It's far more likely that the compensation will come in the form of new opportunities and more work. And that's great, as long as you understand that you're gaining a greater ability to offer whatever it is you've decided to give to achieve your major purpose.

If you're feeling that you're not being adequately compensated now for the work you do, ask yourself why you're doing the work in the first place. If it's just for the paycheck, you're only going to be evaluated in terms of a paycheck. But if you're doing it for something more, as part of a greater purpose, then you'll start to find other rewards. This doesn't mean you shouldn't seek fair financial remuneration, but the Law of Compensation may not be able to offer you anything until you have a clearer understanding of what it is you want.

FAVORABLE ATTENTION

Going the extra mile makes you stand out. The world is packed with people who are happy to do the minimum. They usually get the minimum back. It's like the kid in class who used to raise his hand and ask, "Is this going to be on the midterm?" He wasn't interested in learning. He just wanted to be able to fill in the right circles on the test.

Positive attention comes to you in two major ways when you go the extra mile. First, you gain a reputation for extraordinary work. Superiors remember your efforts, and they entrust bigger responsibilities to you. You get opportunities that less eager people do not. With those responsibilities and opportunities come more chances to display your talents.

Second, your can-do attitude is noticed. You become known as someone who doesn't complain about new tasks and as someone who's willing and eager to roll up your sleeves. You'll gain a reputation as a problem solver, as someone who doesn't complain about a challenge. That will put you in the position to be involved in the new projects, where you'll be the one setting standards for others to meet.

Standing out from the crowd puts you in the position to advance ahead of that crowd. Whether you're a librarian or an entomologist, a pipe-fitter or a PTA member, being recognized for the quality and quantity of your work means that you're treated with more respect and given more freedom. If two people of equal ability are competing for a promotion, the job is going to go to the one who uses his or her abilities more conspicuously and more generously. And why shouldn't it?

INDISPENSABILITY

When going the extra mile is a habit for you, others start to rely on your extraordinary effort. You become a crucial part of their decisions and their operations. You can be indispensable in the very first job you ever have, just as you can become indispensable as a CEO of a Fortune 500 company.

Unfortunately, being indispensable can also go to one's head. But it won't happen to you if you're paying attention and keeping the proper attitude. You can't use your position as an integral part of an organization to make demands. You're not making yourself valuable so that you can be a petty tyrant. If you exploit your importance, others will quickly imagine a world without you. Once they imagine it, they'll find a way to make it real.

Concentrate your efforts on becoming indispensable in the most satisfying and exciting parts of your job. Don't lock yourself into responsibilities that you dislike or that might hold you back. This will poison your efforts to go the extra mile because you'll come to feel that your extra work and service are placing a limit on you. Set your aim high so that people can imagine you being even more indispensable after a promotion.

And always keep in mind the people who are working to be indispensable to you. Don't resent them for this effort: encourage it! Dispense rewards as you can to

You can't reach higher and higher without forcing yourself to grow.

these deserving people, and you'll only encourage them to work harder on your behalf. This will free you to become more important to those who have a role to play in your own advancement.

SELF-IMPROVEMENT

When you've decided that you'll always go the extra mile, you approach every task with a determination to do it better than you've ever done it before. You don't make this choice because somebody's going to give you a gold star. You make it because you know that it's the best possible way to increase your ability to do your work.

You can't reach higher and higher without forcing yourself to grow. You have to keep examining yourself, looking for weaknesses, and reinforcing your strengths. As you do this, you'll come to understand that the extra mile is always a little longer every day. But that won't make you weary: it will excite you. You'll have to apply imagination, self-discipline, enthusiasm, and PMA to succeed, and all those qualities will be invigorated by your daily efforts.

I've never known anyone whose plan for success was mapped out on an hour-by-hour basis. There are always

> **Going the extra mile will make you trust your skills and ideas more than you ever have.**

periods when you have to bide some time. You may be waiting for word to get around about the quality of your work. You may have to meet certain professional requirements. You may be taking a break to save money. But what seems like downtime is really just as important as the day you take a licensing test or buy a business.

Going the extra mile ensures that you're always improving. A secretary who is going to night school while going the extra mile during the day is improving herself. A ski instructor who spends the summers going the extra mile as a waiter is improving himself. You may not be using skills that seem essential to attaining your major purpose, but as long as you're going the extra mile, you're improving yourself.

SELF-CONFIDENCE

There's no way you can be improving on a regular basis without becoming more self-confident. It can't happen! Going the extra mile will make you trust your skills and ideas more than you ever have. You'll be seeing the results of their worth every single day you're out there.

OPPORTUNITY

A reputation for going the extra mile is very hard to keep secret. It's such an extraordinary and, unfortunately, rare

quality, that people must talk about it. Word of your dedication will spread, and, sooner or later, you'll find that
you're being offered chances that seemed impossible
when you first began to dream.

Opportunity may come calling in the form of a job re-
cruiter. It could be a phone call from a new client, a shot at
a research grant, or an assignment in a place you've always
wanted to work. The manifestation of opportunity is often
the result of a combination of the Laws of Increasing Returns and Compensation, as well some favorable attention.
But because it's so essential to enacting your plan for success, it's worth stressing as a benefit by itself.

Some opportunities may be predictable, such as a promotion or a job offer. Others may seem to come out of
the blue. For example, Napoleon Hill once offered free
lectures at a friend's restaurant, and in the audience was a
high-powered executive whose acquaintance led to a valuable opportunity to lecture and write.

When opportunities come, you'll have to evaluate
them. Resist the temptation to say "yes!" simply because
it's exciting to get the offer. It's too easy to be sidetracked
from your plan this way. You should, of course, feel free
to change your plan, but please make that choice only
because you know that it's something you want very
deeply.

Opportunity doesn't only knock once: it isn't a random event. It's something you create through hard work.
Realize that by going the extra mile, you've prepared
yourself for many opportunities. If you choose consciously to let one pass, you'll find others, and they may

be even better for you. Remember, you and your attitude are the true sources of opportunity.

GUMPTION

The search for ways in which you can go the extra mile requires you to think hard and to act decisively. And the longer that you keep up this habit, the more you'll need to employ these qualities. Together, they force you to be very active: active in the extra work you do and active in finding more and more of it.

> **Remember, you and your attitude are the true sources of opportunity.**

This propensity toward action is crucial to your chances for success. Your whole plan means nothing if you aren't out there making it happen. It's very easy to let things slide and to think that you'll get around to something tomorrow. But that attitude always leads to failure.

When you're examining every detail of your work and asking yourself what can be done better, you're giving yourself a daily challenge, and then rising to it. This transforms you into a go-getter. It also makes you into a no-quitter. You don't rest on your accomplishments. You see them as something to surpass, and that outlook carries you forward. It means that you're taking risks, challenging the status quo, and doing things no one else has tried.

This all comes from going the extra mile. You simply can't act on this idea and be the kind of person who lets things slide. You see things through and become the one who make things happen. That's gumption, and you're going to have it in spades.

WALKING THE WALK

Let's suppose you have a very regimented job in a place where innovation is discouraged, and there's no atmosphere that promotes initiative. We'll call this place Doldrums Inc. How do you go the extra mile in a company that practically begs you to sit still?

1. Show up early. Be at your desk an hour before your assigned time and start working. Don't call special attention to this change, just use the time to accomplish what needs to be done. You'll quickly find that your work goes more smoothly and that you have time left at the end of the day to accomplish even more.
2. Identify something that needs to be done and do it. You don't have to reorganize the company filing system or anything else major. Just find a routine task that's waiting for a worker and begin.
3. When you've gotten a grip on this job, look for a way to do it better. If it requires a change in procedures, seek approval from the right person. Don't enter this conversation with the goal of calling attention to your responsibility for the work. Make the discussion about the benefit that will come from the change.
4. Implement the change, and then examine its effects. Find some area affected by what you've done, and examine it with the same attitude you had the first time.

You don't want to showcase yourself; you want to make an improvement.

By this point, Doldrums Inc. will have an idea that you're something special. They may find this confusing, but if your attitude is simply improving how things happen, people won't be too flummoxed. Your changes may surprise a few of your coworkers, but don't be drawn into discussions about what your ulterior motives are. You're doing this solely for the sake of efficiency.

5. At this point, you'll be able to look at your own work with a sharper eye. Find something you do routinely, and do it better. It can be something very small, but concentrate on this thing. Get it accomplished, and then look for the next obvious step.

6. By now, people will be asking you questions about what you're doing. They will be interested in why your reports are more to the point or why you've reduced the number of calls to the customer-service department. Share your ideas without expecting anything in return. This means everything from a compliment to a promotion. Your only reason for applying yourself this way is to learn how to do it better.

After this, you won't be struggling for ways to go the extra mile. You will have added to the number of things you need to do in the day, but you'll be working more efficiently and more happily. Don't look over your shoulder for something good to happen to you. You're already benefiting from your new attitude in the way that you approach your job. Other good things will follow, but at their own pace. A watched pot never boils, and the Laws of Increasing Returns and Compensation follow their own schedules.

You may not work in a company that is anything like Doldrums Inc. You may spend your entire day taking care of your family or driving from one sales call to the next. But it doesn't matter. Begin by identifying something that calls out for improvement, and then give it your full attention. Don't skimp on any of your other responsibilities. Add to them. Don't send telegrams announcing your new attitude. Let it speak for itself. The important thing is making the extra mile a habit for yourself.

Chapter 12

Thinking Like a Boss

"That which you think today, becomes that which you are tomorrow."

—Napoleon Hill

Who's in charge of your life? Oh, you may think that you are, but I wonder if it's true. Are you working just to pay bills? Are you doing a job you hate? Does your day disappear into a long list of routine and uninteresting tasks? Does it feel like a victory when you finally get to take care of something that is important to you?

We all have responsibilities. If there's a way to never have to pay a bill again, I don't know it. Every job has details that are boring. It's impossible to avoid uninteresting and unpleasant chores. But the real question is, whose priorities are getting the most attention?

Until you're able to make sure that you're choosing what has to be done and when to do it, you're going to have a very hard time reaching your goals. You can be in the perfect job, making a great salary, and getting strong support from your coworkers. But if you're not setting the agenda, you're not going to be satisfied. You have to start thinking and acting as if you're in charge of your life. If you don't, external forces will always keep you confined to a routine in which your needs get the last priority.

Becoming the boss of your own life doesn't mean that you turn into a selfish person who never has time to spare for anyone else. It doesn't eliminate obligations that are undeniably yours to fulfill. But it forces you to rethink what's going on in your life and to choose, whenever possible, what happens when. Often, it means taking on new responsibilities. And being the boss of your life makes it much more likely that your effort and hard work will pay off the way you want them to.

> **Properly directed, personal initiative turns even the most timid and lazy person into a dynamic, action-oriented paragon of accomplishment.**

PERSONAL INITIATIVE

Napoleon Hill called thinking like a boss *personal initiative*. He stressed the importance of seeking an opportunity or a need, and then setting out to fulfill it. Properly directed, personal initiative turns even the most timid and lazy person into a dynamic, action-oriented paragon of accomplishment. The real question is how you use personal initiative in your quest for your major purpose.

Personal initiative needs to be applied on two levels. First, on a day-by-day, task-by-task level, you must strive to accomplish all you can in an orderly manner that sets you apart from the people around you. And, second, you must make sure that on a large scale, your efforts are bringing you closer to what you want.

This chapter follows the lesson on going the extra mile because personal initiative is very closely related to the effort to provide more and better service every chance you get. But it's not exactly the same. Going the extra mile primes your thinking to use personal initiative, but thinking like a boss is a more focused, more deliberate approach. You can go the extra mile for a complete stranger you'll never meet again. Thinking like a boss requires a larger goal and more information.

DAY BY DAY

Whether you work for yourself, for a company, or to take care of your family, you can use personal initiative to alter the nature of how your day is spent. Making these changes helps you on two fronts. First, it allows you to make certain that important things happen first. Second, it gives you the skills to examine your life and your work on a bigger scale so that you can begin working toward what you really want.

Begin by making a list of all your tasks done during a typical day so that you get an accurate idea of what you need to do. Now divide all the items into your list into three categories: Crucial, Useful, and Low Priority.

As you make these divisions, you'll need to think hard about where some things go. Crucial things cause big problems if you don't accomplish them. Useful things can be satisfying to accomplish, but they generally don't cause the world to halt in its tracks if you omit them. Low-Priority tasks are routine, mundane things you've fallen into doing, maybe because no one else takes care of them, or because they're just habits.

As busy as you are, the number one enemy of personal initiative isn't lack of time—it's procrastination. Look at the items on your Crucial list. Ask yourself what prevents you from tackling them first thing in the morning. If some scheduling issue prevents doing them, then ask whether you're attending to them at the first opportunity. If your boss was organizing your day, when would these tasks be done? (If you don't have a boss, pretend you are explaining your schedule to some superior.)

Procrastination is easiest when it comes to tasks you dislike. Find the crucial thing you hate most, and do it first. Follow it with the next most-hated crucial thing, and so on. The point of this kind of order to your day is not to fill your morning with drudgery. You're eliminating the procrastination habit and thereby creating time for things you enjoy.

When you've gone through all the Crucial items, look at the Useful list. Consider whether any of these things would be more time-consuming if you did them every other day. Look for things that you formerly used to avoid doing on your Crucial list. You may also discover that some things under Useful are eliminated or dropped down to Low Priority by strict attention to the Crucial items. (Regular, prompt attention to Crucial items also tends to reduce their number.)

There may be some items under Useful that you were using to compensate yourself for the hated items on your Crucial list. With your new dedication, you may be able to cut a few of these Useful tasks from your schedule, or at least reduce their frequency.

When it comes to Low Priority, delegate and eliminate. Look for subordinates, family members, or service providers who can take on these jobs. Can your assistant return phone calls and answer routine correspondence? What would it cost you to have a bookkeeper write checks once a month? And maybe it's time for someone else to host the Neighborhood Watch meetings once in a while.

These examples are only meant to provoke you to think about what your priorities are. If you love a low-priority chore, don't give it up. Personal satisfaction isn't the enemy of personal initiative. You'll probably have to experiment with your schedule, negotiate responsibilities with your boss, and discover whether a delegated job is being done well enough.

But taking a hard look at where your time and energy are going can be intensely revealing. If you discover some unpleasant truths about the way you're working, don't beat yourself up. Look for solutions and don't be afraid to implement them. Don't stick with an unsatisfactory change just for the sake of proving you have initiative, either. You're making changes for your own benefit, not for the sake of change itself.

METAMORPHOSIS

Napoleon Hill distinguished three types of people. The first never succeed because they don't do what they are told to do. The second fail because they *only* do what they are told to do. It's the third group who get what they want in life. They do what needs to be done

Personal initiative makes even average skills extraordinary.

without being told, and they do it better than they're expected to do.

Clearly, you want to be in this third group.

Becoming someone who knows what needs to happen and then accomplishes it on his or her own in an excellent way creates success. It's simply not enough to be good. You must be extraordinary. You don't need to be the smartest, the most imaginative, the most talented, or the most well connected. All these qualities are useless if you don't apply them. You need to be the person who knows how to put himself in the right place at the right time. Personal initiative makes even average skills extraordinary.

Personal initiative teaches you to apply all your assets, as well as how to compensate for weakness. It makes you active in promoting your own cause, creates attention for your efforts, and puts you in the position of seizing the right opportunities. It carries you past disappointments, activates your imagination, and shows you how best to employ the skills and work of other people.

There will always be people who tell you what to do. Listen only to them, and you'll find that your whole day is used up by assigned tasks. Your boss, your family, and your friends will bury you under a list of tasks that satisfy their needs. And the more they come to understand that you're an easy vehicle for getting what they need, the more assigned tasks you'll find yourself doing.

Personal initiative begins when you start assigning your tasks to yourself. They will still involve the needs of other people; but the needs you'll be satisfying will be balanced by needs of your own. You may say no to some requests. You may complete others with an eye to your own requirements. But as soon as you begin thinking about the whole lot of them, and asking how they're important, you'll begin to have some control over what is done and why.

You always need a long view with personal initiative. At work, you must take care of your responsibilities to keep your job. But you can always do this in a way that brings you benefits. If you start finishing things faster and doing them better, you'll take some pressure off yourself and get some favorable attention from higher up. This can mean promotions and more responsibilities, but it also means more independence and more authority.

Have you ever wondered why your boss was so hung up about detail work that just seemed to bog you down? You'll start thinking differently if you contemplate what your perspective would be if you ran the department or the company. You'd gain a new appreciation for tasks that just seem like busywork. Well, you are the boss in your own life. If your adventure is going to be successful, you need to start addressing all the little details as if they matter. Because they do matter—to you.

When you begin thinking like the boss of your own life, you'll probably discover some things about the work you do for others. This will allow you to do the work better, but it may also give you some ideas about how to change things. The changes may be small and incremental, or big and sweeping. Take the time to think through any implications, and then start a discussion about the benefits you've identified.

Thinking like a boss encourages your bosses and your coworkers to treat you with greater respect. They come to understand that you're not just looking to shift work to someone else. They'll take you seriously and listen longer and more closely to what you have to say. You won't find that every suggestion you make is implemented, but don't let that bother you. Listen to the feedback you get, and incorporate it into your thinking. You may learn that accurate information is prized over speedy reports, or that compliance with legal regulations is more complicated than you understood.

Some organizations are more open to initiative than others. Go slow at first, and let other people know that you're most interested in improving things, not in just getting your own way. Your contributions may spark ideas in other people. Don't let this threaten you. If someone else has a better idea, admit it happily. You're not trying to rule the world. Especially at first, you're most concerned with changing your own way of thinking.

Eventually, though, you're going to reach a point where you assume a leadership position or gain more independence. Personal initiative will be more important than ever. Be certain that your own assertiveness isn't squashing input from others. Seek suggestions and weigh them carefully. When you decide to act, however, be certain that you're willing to accept responsibility if something doesn't work out.

Responsibility comes along with initiative. When you make decisions based on your own priorities, you have to accept that risks, complications, and failures are yours along with the benefits. In any organization, the people who are willing to carry their weight are much more valuable than those who simply throw it around. Shirk responsibility for your initiative, and you'll encourage others to limit it.

Admitting responsibility, on the other hand, means that you come out of a bad situation in the best possible light. People who place trust in you will be willing to do it again when they know that you can identify, acknowledge, and correct your errors without being forced to do so. You'll also find that a willingness to acknowledge your own mistakes allows you to correct them before they multiply. Hide from bad news, and you give disaster time to multiply. Confront trouble, and you nip it in the bud. It may sound like an oxymoron when I say that taking responsibility for failure is liberating, but it's much worse to spend your time hiding from the consequences of an unfortunate decision.

You can turn a mistake into an opportunity for promotion with personal initiative. The honesty and willingness to face the music that come along with this quality put you in an excellent position to do this. When the pressure is on, the people upstairs look for someone who thinks fast with the right priorities.

Personal initiative begins small and never stops growing. It shapes your daily actions in such a way that you always know you're making progress toward your goals. It brings you freedom—even when it seems that everyone else in the world is your boss—and even the time you spend exercising it on behalf of someone else's goals starts to yield benefits for you.

> **When the pressure is on, the people upstairs look for someone who thinks fast with the right priorities.**

The greatest among these benefits is a sense of accomplishment. That reward will be yours long before anyone else recognizes your initiative, and it will stay with you from job to job, hour to hour. What can stand in your way when you know how to recognize what needs to be done and you know that you can find a way to do it?

Chapter 13

Becoming Mentally Fit

"An idle mind is the devil's playground."

—Napoleon Hill

I was browsing at the corner newsstand one day when it occurred to me that something was missing. Just about every one of the so-called fitness magazines had a line on the cover promoting a new miracle diet that promised to make me lean and buff in a week. There were so many physical fitness magazines that I figured that if I bought them all, I would get a workout just carrying them home.

What I didn't see was a single promise of mental fitness. Millions of dollars and countless hours of effort were being expended by magazine publishers to convince me that I could reshape my physique. But nobody was trying at all to compel me to buy something in the interest of reshaping my mind. I think there's a real opportunity here for someone to step in and make a fortune with a magazine called Sharp Thinking or Cerebral Focus.

There's nothing wrong with so much being written about toning up your body. But why, I wonder, is such little attention being paid to showing us how to make our minds more powerful? The cynical side of me recognizes that clear-thinking consumers might not attract as many advertisers, but I still see a real need out there to show people how to make their minds as lean, flexible, and strong as our bodies are supposed to be.

Mental fitness is every bit as important as physical fitness. It might not lower your percentage of body fat, but it does something far more important: it helps you master two important principles of success. These principles, accurate thinking and controlled attention, are the equivalents of aerobic and strength fitness. They give you clarity and stamina in the pursuit of your major purpose. Just as a marathoner needs conditioning and endurance to make it to the distant goal, you need mental sharpness and concentration to make it to yours.

The further you go toward realizing your ambitions, the more decisions you're going to have to make. You'll be allocating time, money, and energy to things such as deciding whether to open a branch office, buy a new home, raise money for a new playground at school, or begin working in new media. Even if you have the most detailed plan for success imaginable, you'll still face a constant need to evaluate situations and information. It's an inevitable sign of progress.

Every one of those decisions can be crucial. You can make a big leap forward or send yourself reeling backward, depending on the accuracy of the choice you make. It only makes sense, then, to equip yourself with the mental skills to make good decisions. You want a mind that is capable of cutting to the heart of an issue, recognizing what is at stake, and selecting the course of action that will bring you what you want and need. For that, you need accurate thinking and controlled attention.

The first of these principles, accurate thinking, rests on a two-step process. First, you separate fact from fiction. Second, you sort the remaining facts into the important and the unimportant. Then, and only then, do you begin the decision-making process.

FACT VS. FICTION

We now live in the Information Age. Some call it the Too-Much-Information Age. There is simply no end to the number of so-called authorities, each with their own books, blogs, and websites, and fully financed studies who are ready to tell us everything they think we need to know. On top of that, email has made it possible for everybody to disseminate their ideas without even spending money on paper and postage. There are more television stations than ever, and they're all trying to attract viewers at the expense of everything else, including, sometimes, accuracy.

When you encounter information, be prepared to ask some hard questions:

1. Who is providing it? Do they have a reason for wanting this information to be true? It could be a motive for profit, a philosophical viewpoint, or just the need to be contrary.
2. What is the source of the information? Be suspicious of unnamed sources or vague attributions such as "a reliable authority" or the infamous "well-known fact."

3. Does it agree with other things you know to be true? You need to be particularly careful in this assessment. The world does change, but keep in mind that something that seems too good to be true often is. The same goes for bad news. There are people out there who relish spreading bad news.

4. How can you verify it? Is there a higher authority? Can you go straight to the source to confirm what you've been told?

5. What isn't being said? People often shape news to their own purposes by omitting details that don't suit their purpose in spreading a story.

Answering these questions will winnow out a huge amount of the information you encounter. You may not be able to dismiss the information as outright lies, but it will prevent you from accepting as fact things that are nothing more than rumors or hype. Recognize that there is a hazy, gray realm where fact and fiction mingle. No lie seems as true as the one based on a truth. You don't want to accept a "fact" that is merely a cleverly disguised fiction.

Let's walk through a situation where someone encounters some information that seems significant to their purpose in life. This will show you how the evaluation process works so that you can get a good idea of what to look out for when separating fact from fiction.

Marisol is the director of a community arts center. The center exhibits the work of local painters and other artists, as well as stages several plays throughout the year, including an annual Shakespeare play performed free in the park across the street during the summer. One evening, at the opening of a new exhibition, she is talking to the husband of one of the artists. He owns a construction company and tells her he has just won a contract to build a memorial to war veterans in the park. He says it will go smack in the middle of the site where the stage is erected for the Shakespeare play.

Marisol has just received information. It has the potential to be very disruptive to one of her center's most popular events, and, if it's true, she'll need to adjust her plans immediately. She sees a city council member across the room and is tempted to go ask some pointed questions about why she wasn't told this was happening. Instead, she begins asking herself the five questions above.

1. Who is providing it? Marisol recognizes that this man should know whether he has won a contract or not. He might be bragging, trying to get some attention for himself while his wife is being complimented on her pottery, but he's not likely to be lying, given that Marisol will soon be able to see whether or not the memorial is constructed.

2. What is the source of the information? Marisol realizes that she can call the city parks department in the morning to confirm the information. They will have the last word on whether construction will be going ahead. The contractor is a good source, but the parks department will be better.

3. Does it agree with other things you know to be true? Before now, Marisol hasn't heard about plans for a

war memorial. But she does know that the center has a contract with the parks department to stage the show, and that it runs for two more years. This tells her that some pieces of the puzzle are clearly still missing.

4. How can you verify it? A call to the parks department will tell her everything. Marisol decides it will be the first thing she does in the morning. She won't do anything else about this news until she can get verification.

5. What isn't being said? In her conversation with the parks department the next morning, Marisol learns that she was only given part of the story. Yes, a memorial is being built on the site where the plays have been produced. But, thanks to a donation from a local businesswoman, a new, permanent stage is being constructed in another part of the park. And construction on either project won't begin until the fall, so there will be no disruption to this year's play. The parks department is actually glad that Marisol called because they were about to ask for her suggestions about the design of the new stage. She schedules a meeting with them, and goes back to her other duties with a load off her mind.

If Marisol had gone stomping across the room as soon as she heard about the memorial, she could have easily embarrassed herself by acting on incomplete information. Challenging a city council member with only half the story would have made her look rash and uncooperative. Instead, she evaluated what she heard and took the information lightly until she was able to verify it. In the process, she learned that what had seemed like bad news was actually good. The contractor wasn't being malicious, just a little petty by not telling her the entire story. Marisol later learned that he had lost the bid on the stage, so it wasn't surprising he didn't bring it up.

Sometimes it's not possible to answer all five of these questions immediately or on your own. If information has important implications for your plans, don't hesitate to take time to investigate further, as Marisol did. Fact-checking is also an area where your Master Mind alliance can be enormously useful. Because a Master Mind alliance is composed of people of different skills, don't hesitate to go to a member with expertise in a subject where you're not as knowledgeable.

Don't spread information around that you don't know to be true. If you're seeking confirmation, present yourself that way. If you gain a reputation as a gossip or boaster, you'll only attract other people interested in telling the latest tales. You'll be overwhelmed by fantastic and scandalous stories, and soon your head will be full of lots of useless misinformation. You don't want that. Not only is it distracting, but it also makes other accurate-thinking people suspicious and less willing to share good information with you or help you sort fact from fiction.

The separation is only half the process. Once you know what is true and what is not, you still have to decide whether the facts at hand are meaningful. There are plenty of facts out there. The question that remains is whether they matter.

IMPORTANT VS. UNIMPORTANT

Any bookstore can sell you an almanac. Hundreds of pages packed with statistics from assorted agencies tell you everything from the gross national product of India to the population of Benton County, Oregon. If you memorized an almanac, you could probably make a fortune on the game shows, although people would avoid you at parties. What you would not do is help yourself attain what you want most in life. Facts, by themselves, are useless things. They have to be applied properly to have any value, and proper application begins with deciding whether a fact is significant to what you're doing.

This determination begins with a clear understanding of your purpose in life. Knowing your major purpose provides the basic framework for evaluating the importance of information. You'll learn many facts every day. Some of them may be very interesting, but the first question you need to ask is whether they have an impact on what you're doing. But even facts that seem to have a direct bearing on your major purpose can be unimportant. Usually, in a cluster of facts, just one or two are truly important to your plans. You simply have to understand where your priorities lie.

Being in touch with what is important to you makes choices clearer. When you have a crystallized idea of what you want and how you plan to get it, you'll find that choices are more obvious, though not necessarily easier or without consequences. Evaluating consequences and deciding what is important to you is simpler when you know what you need and what you're willing to live with for the sake of your goals. When you know what your pri-

When you know what your priorities are, you won't find yourself stumped by the inability to make a choice.

orities are, you won't find your-self stumped by the inability to make a choice.

The clarity that comes with ac-curate thinking prepares you for the second element of mental fit-ness: controlled attention. Con-trolled attention is a powerful idea, but it isn't very useful to you until you've developed accurate thinking, for the simple reason that you must know what you want to concentrate your attention on be-fore you can truly make it pay off. Let's take a look at ex-actly what controlled attention is and how you can use it.

CONTROLLED ATTENTION

Napoleon Hill often referred to this principle by another name: *concentration*. Put simply, controlled attention is

Ironically, focusing your conscious thinking is the best way to put your versatile subconscious mind to work.

focusing all your thinking on a single idea or question. This focus activates several mental faculties and directs them to begin creat-ing the result that you need. Your imagination and your enthusi-asm play a big role, but so does your subconscious mind. Ironi-cally, focusing your conscious thinking is the best way to put your versatile subconscious mind to work.

Your subconscious is the back burner of your mind. It's the place where your ideas take on a life of their own. This can be good or bad, depending on the nature of the ideas that are bubbling away back there. Fears thrive in your subconscious, but so does inspiration. From the beginning of this book, you've been learning techniques to eliminate some of the negative things that can take root in your subconscious. You've been replacing them with beneficial thoughts and ideas.

PMA is the most potent of the ways in which you keep your subconscious free of harmful ideas. But the things you've learned about enthusiasm, imagination, applied faith, and self-discipline also serve to impress your subconscious with the importance of your major purpose and the skills you need to attain it.

It might seem that your subconscious mind is that part of you that isn't responsive to direction, but this isn't so. Your subconscious works on its own, but it does so in response to the stimulus that you give it. It doesn't create ideas out of whole cloth; it begins from the raw material that you provide it through your conscious thoughts.

Suppose that while walking down your block, a big dog comes running at you, barking and with its teeth bared. Even if the owner calls it off before it gets near you, you'll have a quick, sudden impression of danger. That impression will arise in your conscious mind, but it will enter your subconscious as well.

What happens next will depend on how you direct your conscious mind. If you scurry on about your business with your heart racing, and you keep dwelling on the danger you faced, your subconscious mind is going to recognize this threat as something significant. You'll spend the rest of the day with the jitters. And worse, in the days that follow, every time you come near the yard where the dog is, you're going to feel anxiety again. This anxiety will grow stronger, and soon, other dogs will start to seem intimidating.

But this isn't your only option. If you consciously respond to the threat by focusing your mind on the fact that you weren't attacked and that you are indeed safe, your subconscious won't obsess about the dog. Even better, if you take the time to make friends with the dog and its owner, you'll be impressing your subconscious with the idea that unfriendly creatures can become friendly with the right approach.

You can see from this example why the right attitude toward a setback or threat is important. If you impress your subconscious with the idea that you've failed at something, the idea of failure begins to take root. If, instead, you impress your subconscious with the need for a solution and with determination to succeed, those ideas will be what your subconscious mind dwells on.

Vigorous PMA serves as a guardian of your subconscious, keeping unpleasant ideas out and providing a steady store of good impressions. Acting on applied faith is another very effective means of directing your subconscious, for your deeds as well as your thoughts will make an impression. But the crux of controlled attention is making a specific, determined effort to impress your subconscious with a goal or idea, so that it begins to work on creating what you need.

Controlled attention is essentially a form of self-hypnosis. I know that hypnosis is a loaded term. Mention it, and people think of those Las Vegas shows where audience members are convinced they are a teapot or a chicken. But controlled attention isn't about getting laughs. It's a means of transforming your ideas about yourself and reality.

You've already been engaging in it. Every time you read your statement of purpose, you're directing your conscious and your unconscious minds to focus on your major purpose and how you'll attain it. This is why you should read it repeatedly throughout the day to keep the impression fresh and to allow it to color all your thoughts and actions.

The triggers and sparks you use to combat bad habits and fire up your enthusiasm are also forms of controlled attention and, thus, hypnosis. This is why they become stronger each time you use them: they become more deeply embedded in your thoughts.

You can use controlled attention in specific circumstances to affect your thoughts and actions. You can solve a problem or change a habit that you've spent a lifetime acquiring.

Problem-solving through controlled attention begins with the application of accurate thinking. You need to identify clearly the problem that you face. It's useful to write down the issue in a single sentence to help pare away unimportant details. An example would look something like this:

I need to overcome my competitor's price advantage.

(Note that I haven't specified a particular solution to the problem in the statement. I might have some ideas about quality, service, or payment terms, but I don't want to slant or prejudice the results. I have also placed myself in the statement, since I want a solution that will come from my own actions. I don't want to suggest to myself that this is someone else's problem to solve.)

Now, find a quiet place where you won't be interrupted and make sure you have some time to devote. Fifteen minutes will get the process off to a good start.

Read the statement aloud to yourself ten times, and focus all your thoughts on this idea. By the tenth time, you'll have already given your subconscious a resoundingly strong impression that this is something significant. You will also have sent a message to your imagination, and it will kick into gear.

Let yourself muse on the problem. Scribble down ideas as they come to you. If your imagination catches fire, great. But you shouldn't expect a solution instantly. When you feel you've come to the end of your inspiration, it's okay to stop.

You can repeat this process over the next several days. You may find what you need in one of the sessions. But it's just as likely that the idea will come to you at another moment: in the shower or while driving to work. Your subconscious has unpredictable timing, but it will deliver for you. You may find that something you read or something someone says produces one of those "Eureka!" moments, when suddenly it all becomes clear to you.

Don't be afraid to ask some hard questions about what your subconscious produces. You may have only the beginnings of an answer rather than a whole solution. But what you'll find is that your mind has made some connections that you had overlooked through conscious examination. You're making contact with Infinite Intelligence: sensing a relationship that exists but hasn't been fully explored or understood yet.

You can also adapt this technique to make behavioral changes in yourself. You can improve your attitude toward someone or something, or create a new and beneficial habit. Because attitudes are habits of thought, the process is very similar. Instead of writing out a statement of a problem, write down an expression of the habit you want to cultivate. Give yourself the same kind of quiet time to focus your thinking, and then it's best to follow the focus time with an immediate action based on your new habit.

If you want to be more regular about exercise, focus your thinking right before you work out. If you're eliminating snacking on junk food, you'll know when you're tempted to eat, so focus yourself before you find yourself at the vending machine. If you're increasing your self-confidence, focus yourself before you pick up the phone to make a call you've been dreading. Focusing will become a habit by itself, and along with the new habits you're creating, you'll find that you have the ability to hone in on any important task.

Controlled attention operates very similarly to applied faith because it prepares you to do things that might have otherwise seemed impossible or unlikely. Very often, concentrating your thinking on something you need will result in that something coming your way. This isn't like asking the Universe for a new car: God won't work a miracle for you. But God may help you find a way to work the miracle yourself. Controlled attention is an important part of the great Napoleon Hill adage: whatever you can conceive and believe, you can achieve.

Controlled attention has two applications. First, you can use it to jump everyday hurdles. But, second, when you focus your mind on your major desire, you begin creating all the things you need to make it happen. Accurate thinking will help keep you from being distracted by shiny things that look pretty but aren't important. Controlled attention will let you create the nuts and bolts and iron girders you'll use to achieve your goals.

Make yourself mentally fit and put yourself on the track to what you want.

Napoleon Hill often said that your mind is the one thing you can truly control. If tomorrow you woke up destitute, you could still begin creating and working toward your major purpose before you'd even had a chance to think about breakfast. Your mind is the only essential tool for achieving success. So don't be lazy when it comes to using it. Make yourself mentally fit and put yourself on the track to what you want.

Chapter 14

Creating Harmony

"Harmony in human relationships is a man's greatest asset. Don't permit anyone to rob you of your share."

—Napoleon Hill

Wherever you are, whatever you want most in life, you'll attain it only by working with other people. You need to be effective at inspiring cooperation—and at giving it—if you expect to achieve your major purpose. Competition is part of our society. There's nothing wrong with it. Our free enterprise systems depend on it.

> Civilization advances because people compete, but civilization endures because people cooperate.

It pushes all of us to try harder, to take risks, and to experiment. Civilization advances because people compete, but civilization endures because people cooperate, and healthy competition can take place only because of cooperation. Without a cooperative society, we'd all be fighting for food and shelter, not dreaming the big dreams. Who would create art, discover medical advances, or invent new technology if we all woke up each morning knowing that the most important thing we had to do was find a way to stay alive? No one.

When you become skilled at inspiring cooperation, you'll find that you have more time and resources to devote to reaching your goals. Cooperation takes work and sacrifice, but it's also tremendously liberating. You'll encounter problems and obstacles that you'll surmount only with help from other people, and the single way to be sure that you'll find that help when you need it is being able to inspire cooperation.

Creating the harmony that inspires cooperation—like so many other principles discussed in this book—begins with your attitude. You can develop techniques that will help you, but none of them will be worth much unless your heart and head are in the right place.

PREPARING FOR COOPERATION

A cooperative attitude isn't something you can turn on or off as the situation warrants it. You have to maintain a spirit of cooperation at all times. Being cooperative should be part of your reputation. If people sense that you'll cooperate only when you're going to gain the greatest benefits for yourself, they won't cooperate with you happily and freely. They may work with you when it's absolutely necessary, but their cooperation will end the instant they have what they want.

Offer cooperation generously, on the other hand, and you'll find that people reciprocate. No, not every single person, but more than enough people that you'll be able to create a pool of cooperative spirit, a reservoir of harmonious good feeling that you'll be able to tap as you need it. Even those people who were initially grudging about their cooperation with you may decide that you're worthy of their generosity. One generous person in a group of people who are stingy can begin to alter everyone's attitude toward cooperation.

It's for this reason that you should not be hasty in deciding that someone with whom you've cooperated is stinting on returned cooperation. Some people simply are not used to a generous give-and-take. They may have learned to give no more than is absolutely necessary out of a fear of getting burned. There is no better way to erase their negative ideas about cooperation than to show them a liberal spirit of teamwork whenever possible. As Napoleon Hill often said, "Deeds, not words, will change attitudes."

Especially when you're new to cooperation, or when you're in a new environment, offer your cooperation with little expectation of immediate rewards. Your resulting good reputation will be a reward in itself. This may seem a difficult thing when you're struggling to accomplish all the things you need to do, but it will pay dividends very soon. With a reputation for being willing to help others, you'll find people who are willing to offer you help before you even ask for it, even before you even realize that you need it.

In any organization, leaders look for people they can rely on to carry a greater share of the common burden. There is no shortage of people who shirk responsibility. Mark yourself out as someone who gladly shoulders his share of the load, and you'll find that more experienced people will pay attention to you. Yes, they'll give you more to do, but they'll also give you advice and share information that they don't dispense to people who have demonstrated that they won't make use of it anyway.

As you assume leadership roles, be sure to keep your eyes open for people who, like you, recognize the value of cooperation. Extend a friendly hand to them, and make yourself an ally who will be willing to give maximum effort on your behalf. Don't treat someone with initiative and a cooperative spirit as a threat. So what if that new recruit wants your job someday? By that point, you'll have moved on, and by helping him get there, you'll have created a bond that you may be able to call upon at a crucial moment.

There is no strict quid pro quo in cooperation. You simply can't anticipate exactly what you'll need in the future. You don't want to approach someone for help only to hear that your past services didn't cover this circumstance. You want to inspire open-handed collaboration, and the only way to accomplish this is to be similarly unselfish when it comes to working with others. Don't appear to be doing a cost-benefit analysis when someone proposes something to you. Respond graciously, enthusiastically, and in the affirmative.

There are, however, a few occasions when you'll want to decline cooperation. First, don't let a liberal spirit of teamwork rope you into something inappropriate. If you're asked to do something that strikes you as unethical or that you know would create ill will among other people who are important to you, say no. Be direct in explaining why you're bowing out. Don't try to make an excuse that you're too busy or unable to help. Make it clear why you won't cooperate in this instance.

People who make these kinds of inappropriate proposals do it for one of two reasons. Often, they fail to understand the implications of their actions. You may set someone like this straight, but even if you don't, you'll still leave him or her with the impression that you're cooperative under the right circumstances. There are, however, also people who see nothing wrong with being underhanded. You don't want their cooperation. They will never be willing to offer you the same kind of clear-headed advice that you've given them, and you'll never be sure that in cooperating with you, they are not after something else entirely. Steer clear.

Second, you may sometimes be asked to cooperate in a plan that has obvious flaws. If this is the case, consider first whether you can make a suggestion that will correct the flaw. This is an extremely valuable form of cooperation to give someone. If your suggestion is accepted, feel free to participate. But if you sense that the plan is so obviously bad that it can't be saved, say so. Be tactful in doing it, but don't be shy about revealing the source of your reservations. Again, don't make up an excuse that makes it seem that suddenly you're less generous. It's far better to be known as someone with a sharp mind and firm convictions than as someone who is either unpredictable or vague in explaining their refusal, or who always says yes for the sake of getting along.

The toughest cases are those in which you're asked to cooperate in something that conflicts with your own plans for success. If the distraction is minor, it's probably worth going along. We often give up something to get something more important later. Cooperation is extremely valuable and can pay great dividends in the long run. But there are cases when someone may ask for help that, if given, will cause you a big setback. You may be asked to move, to take a promotion into a different department, or to give up something you've worked very hard to achieve.

If you're faced with the prospect of this kind of sacrifice, you'll have to make a hard decision, taking into account your ability to recover and what it will cost you to say either yes or no. Whatever you decide may have profound implications. It's important to tell whoever is asking for your cooperation exactly what is at stake. This should provide you with a little time to weigh your options and investigate alternatives. You need to know definitively what the costs will be and how, if ever, you can recover. Whatever answer you give, you need to establish your motivations clearly. If you refuse to go along, you'll lessen any ill will by making sure everyone knows exactly what you would have been giving up. Sometimes people are unthinking in asking for great sacrifices, and they may be startled to discover what the cost would have been to you. Even people who know the stakes will appreciate your careful deliberation, though they may still wish you had chosen differently.

If you make a great sacrifice, keep a few things in mind. First, you made it. Don't blame anyone else for the choice. Blaming others is a fast way to poison relationships.

Accept that you've chosen your new situation, and then begin working to move ahead. Second, as you know from dealing with other setbacks, start searching for unseen advantages in your new situation. They are there. The faster you can find them, the faster you can exploit them. And third, don't let this setback quench your spirit of co-operation. There is no faster way to ruin your reputation for generous accommodation than by becoming stingy after someone has asked you for something important, which you gave them. Conversely, there is no better way of becoming known as a generous cooperator than by proceeding with good grace and the same openness to-ward working with others on future projects.

The face you show people when they ask for your cooperation makes all the difference when you ask them in return. Draw on

You help yourself every time you help someone else.

other lessons in this book to provide bountiful coopera-tion when you give it. Respond with PMA, enthusiasm, and imagination. Go the extra mile, act on applied faith, and turn on your pleasing personality. Show initiative in your cooperative work, and approach it with the same mental skills you use for your personal efforts. In this way, you help yourself every time you help someone else.

MOTIVES FOR COOPERATION

You'll want cooperation from a wide range of people, no matter your major purpose. At various points, you'll need help from family members, neighbors, and people at work.

The people at work can be subordinates, colleagues, or superiors. The nature of your relations with all these people will vary, as will the specific tools you'll use to inspire them to work with you. Although your attitude will be the most important factor in convincing anyone to help you, there are a number of techniques you can employ in these circumstances to create and reward cooperation.

It's good at this point to recall Napoleon Hill's list of the ten basic motives for human action. To save you from flipping back to Chapter 3, here they are again:

1. Self-preservation
2. Love
3. Fear
4. Sex
5. Desire for life after death
6. Freedom, mental and physical
7. Anger
8. Hate
9. Desire for recognition and self-expression
10. Wealth

You can use any of these motives as the basis for a cooperative relationship, although they have different advantages and costs.

SELF-PRESERVATION

This is a high-stakes motive, even when you're dealing with the perception of a threat, rather than the actual risk of death. People who believe that their way of life or earning a living is at risk will often react just as if their very lives were in play, simply because they can't envision living except as they do now. From these beliefs, you gain tremendous motivation and a willingness to take risks and make tough choices. But you must also be aware that desperation can lead people into making rash decisions and cloud their ability to think things through.

When you make an appeal to cooperation based on self-preservation, it's important that you craft your approach carefully. Offer a vision with positive results: don't offer only the elimination of a threat. Present the hope of a better situation, so that you provide people with something to hope for. People who are worried about self-preservation need guidance and leadership. You and your allies should emerge from your struggle stronger and more determined, not weakened and weary.

LOVE

Asking for cooperation on the basis of love carries particular responsibilities. This applies both to situations when it's love for you that underlies the cooperation, as well as to when someone else is the object of affection. People will often do more for love of another than they will do for themselves.

If you inspire cooperation on the basis of love, keep in mind that you must be realistic in what you ask for and in what you expect to happen. You can't hold out the hope of attaining love where it doesn't exist, and you especially can't make or imply the promise of someone else's love in exchange for cooperation. Be aware also that if love sours or falters, your cooperation will be severely weakened.

On the other hand, cooperation born of love can weather the worst storms and setbacks. While this is enormously satisfying and can even strengthen the love between two people, be careful not to take the affection for granted. There is nothing wrong with being greatly appreciative of the help you gain on the basis of love. The cost to you is minimal, and even if you fail at what you set out to do, a stronger love relationship is never a consolation prize.

FEAR

Fear makes people irrational. Don't attempt to create fear in order to win cooperation. However, sometimes fear exists on its own and is part of why people will agree to work with you. Be certain that your cooperation is founded on a means of eliminating the source of someone's fears and doesn't simply exploit the fear itself.

If you use fear as a whip for driving someone to cooperate with you, you'll create an almost indestructible association in their minds between you and whatever they fear. They will be resentful and withholding, and you'll gain only grudging help, if any. As soon as the threat is eliminated, you may be next on that person's list for elimination.

On the other hand, if you help someone cope with a fear, offering guidance and support, you'll be strengthening your ally and creating a bond that will last long past the task you face together. People motivated by fear often need a good deal of direction because they want the fastest way out, no matter the cost. You'll need to appear strong and confident as you work together, which begins with making sure that you acknowledge and overcome any fears you may have yourself.

SEX

Offering or seeking sex to win cooperation is a formula for disaster. You should not expect or want cooperation on the basis of sexual interest, and you certainly don't want to make sex a requirement of any working relationship. If you want to develop a fling into something more meaningful, let it grow of its own accord, and don't stake your major purpose on something casual and shallow.

DESIRE FOR LIFE AFTER DEATH

Religious motivations can inspire deep and lasting cooperation, but they do require a great deal of alignment between your beliefs and those of the people you work with. It would be extremely manipulative to draw someone into false cooperation on the basis of religion, and you'd deserve nothing less than having it fail.

Yet religiously inspired altruism leads people to do extraordinary things. If you make an appeal to someone on this basis, do it fair and square. If your ideas in other areas don't jibe, make that clear so they can make choices with their eyes wide open. Keep in mind that you'll never be able to proceed without fully respecting your partner's beliefs, and recognize that you may have to make some concessions to avoid causing a conflict of convictions.

Keep in mind that your own desire for life after death may not follow the same code as someone else's. Don't use a cooperative relationship to proselytize or insist on ideas that have little to do with your common goal. If you're successful in reaching across a divide of beliefs, let the cooperation between you stand as an example of what your faith can accomplish. Deeds, as always, will speak louder than a sermon.

FREEDOM

Great things have been won by people cooperating in the name of physical and mental freedom. This lofty motive often brings out the best in people, inspiring them to work long and hard, and to sacrifice much. You owe your greatest respect and support to anyone who works with you from this motivation.

Keep in mind that the desire for freedom can be disguised by other apparent motivations. An urge for wealth is often driven by the desire for freedom, and self-preservation and freedom often appear together as joint motives. Get to know the people with whom you're cooperating so that you understand what is most important to them.

Cooperation can come hard to someone who struggles for freedom; if you encounter resistance to cooperation, ask yourself whether someone is worried about surrendering too much independence. Make sure that your offer of cooperation doesn't appear to ask people to give up something essential. If the cooperation begins, take particular care that you don't make unilateral decisions, and keep lines of communication open and active. People motivated by the desire for freedom are worthy allies if you can win them over.

ANGER

People can be angry about an issue without that anger being their primary motivation. This is fine. Anger is sometimes a wholly acceptable, even worthy, response to a problem or situation. However, when anger lies at the root of someone's cooperation with you, you're usually in for trouble.

People motivated by the desire for freedom are worthy allies if you can win them over.

People motivated by anger are sometimes out for revenge, and their ideas and efforts will be almost uniformly destructive. They will be difficult to cooperate with without giving up some things that are very important to you, such as honesty and PMA, and they will dislike any attempt you make to be reasonable. They want emotional satisfaction at any cost.

Talk with someone who seems motivated by anger. See if some larger, more worthy goal than payback is motivating them. If you can find it, build your cooperation around that goal and not the idea of revenge. It may not work out on the first try, but stay willing to come back and broach the subject again when tempers are a little cooler.

If you discover that anger has overwhelmed someone you're cooperating with, be prepared to pull back rather than be drawn into something messy. You can be tarred with the same brush if an ally does something rash, and you need to make it clear that your goals have diverged. The anger may pass quickly, in which case, you can resume cooperation, but don't simply rush back into the relationship. Ask hard questions. Be plainspoken about what concerns you. Someone still in the grips of anger will betray himself or herself. Someone who is over it will be able to answer honestly, and you'll both be able to get back to work.

HATE

Stay away from this motive. It poisons everything. Don't use it. End cooperation with people driven by it. The smartest, wealthiest, most imaginative person in the world isn't worth having as an ally if motivated by hate.

RECOGNITION AND SELF-EXPRESSION

You can begin satisfying these motives as soon as you begin cooperating with someone. Offer praise and provide someone with the chance to express himself or herself in your relationship, and you'll win an eager ally quickly.

Keep in mind that these motives can lead people astray from an agreed-upon purpose. They may seek fame or intellectual freedom at the expense of whatever goal you've set together. It's best to lay out a very clear plan for proceeding, so that you both know what is most important.

You can use these motives to win help from people who might otherwise have little to gain from your cooperation. The country is full of hospitals, libraries, and theaters that are named after people who got recognition in exchange for a cash donation. You may also find that there are many retired people eager to work on a community project in exchange for the satisfaction of having an impact once more. Be generous in providing what people need to satisfy these motives, and you'll win great skill and talent to your side.

WEALTH

This makes the world go 'round, doesn't it? Financial incentives are a crisply defined way of winning cooperation, and they are used all the time. Businesses are founded on this kind of cooperation, and every one of us must pay at least some attention to keeping money rolling in.

More than with any other kind of motive, you need to define financial costs and rewards as sharply as possible. You can't afford to discover halfway through that someone feels cheated or can't hold up his or her end of an arrangement. If you need money urgently, you may have to accept your rewards in some other form to inspire someone to cooperate with you.

Get good legal and financial advice before embarking on this kind of cooperation. Know what you're getting and what you're giving up. And if things get rocky, be prepared to show that you're making sacrifices first before you ask anyone else to make a sacrifice. Don't make promises that will be impossible to keep, and listen hard when someone asks questions. It's better to hear and act on advice the first time than to show you have to be driven to it.

Financial rewards inspire their own kind of thrill. Watch yourself and your allies to make certain that none of you are letting the motivation for wealth distract you from the process by which you'll create it. Some people are more susceptible to cutting corners than others, and you can't afford a dishonest shortcut when it comes to your major purpose.

There is no motive for human behavior that is without some dangers. People have made mistakes acting on every one of them. When you ask anyone for cooperation, you need to understand the driving force that will lead to an affirmative answer, as well as what risks and costs will be associated with that force. Cooperative relationships are fluid: the motive that binds people to you can change as their needs and priorities shift. Cooperation, therefore, can never be taken for granted. As with anything valuable, it requires maintenance.

HARMONIC TUNE-UPS

Staying alert in any relationship saves you grief. You wouldn't expect a marriage to thrive without effort, and the same applies to bonds that encourage people to work with you. Here are some ways to help keep cooperative efforts strong and healthy so that you can draw on them as you need to, without worrying that you're asking for too much.

Communication

Paying attention to all the details of your plan for success can easily consume all your time if you let it. This is a mistake. Friends and family will resent being treated as if they are only playing supporting roles in the great drama that is your life. Make sure that you allow time, every day, to be in touch with people and to stay acquainted with what is important to them. I don't mean that you sit down and quiz them about what they want in life and the progress they are making. Just spend time at meals, at a movie, relaxing together, or listening to music. The bonds of family and friendship run deeper than spoken words. Simply enjoying someone's company is a valuable gift you give each other. If something important needs to be said, the opportunity is there.

In business relationships, the level of personal interaction will vary. You can have strong cooperative bonds with people whose personal lives you know nothing about. Or you can become great friends as well. But in either case, never assume that what has worked in the past is still working. If you sense any signs of trouble or reluctance, talk about it. The irony of a strong bond is that it can lead people to be hesitant about voicing the need for change. If a cooperative partner holds back, resentment can creep into the bond and grow, unnoticed, until, at a crucial moment, you find that the help you need is too costly to the other person. You don't need these kinds of discoveries. Frequent, open communication will save you much heartache.

Appreciation

Don't be stingy with thanks or praise. Heartfelt thanks for the help someone gives you can often be every bit as valuable as the help you return to them. Give public credit where it's appropriate, and whenever something positive happens to you, make it a priority to share the good news with those who have assisted you. Success has an appeal of its own: when you draw people into your successes, you share the proud moment with them. No one in the whole world feels as if he or she knows the thrill of success too often.

> **Frequent, open communication will save you much heartache.**

Remembering birthdays, anniversaries, and other happy moments also shows you value people and the help they give you. It's common to send cards or gifts at holiday time, and there is nothing wrong with this. But you'll make a stronger impression if you choose another time—it doesn't even have to be a significant date—to drop someone a note or an email that says, very simply, why you treasure your relationship. Formal acknowledgments are becoming rare in today's world, which makes them all the more appreciated. Extravagant gifts are nice, but since they can also seem to impose an obligation, I think you're always better off with deeply felt words. After all, an honestly written paragraph conveys more meaning and more specific regard than a bottle of fine wine or a box of fruit.

Generosity

Although it can seem costly, it's wise to season all your cooperative relationships with a healthy dose of going the extra mile, even those relationships that seem to be thriving on their own. Someone with a manipulative bent would say that this just binds people to you more closely, but I prefer to think of it as keeping your own attitude sufficiently open and giving. Cooperation succeeds or fails based on your mindset. Go the extra mile routinely, and you'll ensure that you're asking, "How are we both better off?" rather than, "What am I getting out of this?"

Discovering that you have a skill for getting people to work with you can be exhilarating. It's exciting to realize just how many people you can forge this kind of bond with and how helpful this cooperation is. And the temptation may grow to see all these helpful people as tools rather than as allies. If you're always looking to give people more than you're getting, you won't succumb to becoming a narcissist who sees the entire world as a machine for satisfying his own urges. The instant you demand, rather than ask, for aid, all the work you've done to inspire cooperation will evaporate.

Always remember that cooperation is something you prepare yourself to receive. There is no right to cooperation. It's a gift that other people offer you. The generosity of others may not be equal to your own, but don't dwell on that. Just keep preparing yourself to get the help you need, and it will arrive.

Chapter 15

Managing Your Resources

"Time and money are precious resources; few people striving for success ever believe they possess either one in excess."

—Napoleon Hill

Whoever you are and whoever you'll become, by now you've grasped just how possible your major purpose is. You know that your plans can become real through your thoughts and deeds. You understand that every day that passes by can bring you closer to what you want from life.

But are there days when you're not so sure that is happening? Days when you feel lucky not to lose ground? Even when you have a plan for success, and you've mastered all the principles you've learned so far, it can be difficult and exasperating to see the sun rise and set on the world without some sense of progress. Most of us don't write plans that work in day-by-day increments, but we all live day by day, so it's worthwhile to take a look at how we can manage things on that basis.

Time and money are both spent daily. While the techniques you use for handling them are not always the same, both require a certain vigilance to prevent them from slipping through your fingers. We all have differing styles when it comes to organizing and using our resources, but no matter how you approach things, it's essential to be fully conscious of your strengths and weaknesses so that you can play to your strong suits and compensate for blind spots.

Before we look at the resource-management issues directly, let's see what style you use so that you can proceed with open eyes and an open mind.

THREE STYLES

Experts have identified many personal approaches to handling your affairs. If you decide to consult any of the very practical and useful books out there, you'll learn a good deal about yourself. However, for our purposes, we can define three broad categories into which everyone falls. There's nothing good or bad about any of these, per se, but each comes with advantages and disadvantages.

Engineers

Engineers are the most tightly organized people around. They love calendars and notebooks. Their schedules are meticulously plotted, they know where everything they own is, and they know how and when they will spend the quarter in the bottom of their pocket. This all works to their good. They are great project managers.

Engineers are most likely to stumble when something interrupts their plans. If one item falls out of order, they have difficulty adapting to the change. Getting reorganized is a huge task because all the pieces have to be rearranged just so until they are comfortable again.

Engineers most need to develop flexibility as an organizing skill.

Improvisers

Improvisers rarely have tightly planned schedules or careful monetary budgets. Instead, they are constantly aware of their most immediate priorities and are very comfortable switching between tasks to see that the hot-button issues are dealt with. They often have very strong people skills because they are sensitive to what's important to others.

Improvisers struggle with long-term progress. They often have the small daily issues well in hand, but it can be difficult for them to translate all those small victories into something larger, simply because they have a hard time switching their focus to issues that aren't pressing.

Improvisers most need to develop long-range planning as an organizing skill.

Theorists

Theorists can plan out intricate schedules and draw up budgets that get the maximum out of the least amount of money. They enjoy this kind of planning, and they do it extremely well. They can be very helpful to organizations for their ability to see a fully designed route to a lofty dream.

However, theorists are almost always struggling to apply their plans in real life. It's not that they have unrealistic goals, just that they get much more satisfaction out of the thinking rather than out of the doing. Procrastination dogs their efforts, and some of them even enjoy replanning once delay has thrown their first scheme off course.

Theorists most need to develop persistence as an organizational skill.

It isn't important that you decide at this moment which of these three groups you fall into. Maybe you're a hybrid. And even if you're a Theorist with Improviser overtones, it won't hurt you to pay close attention when I discuss flexibility. None of the qualities you need for good organization appears full blown in any one of these groups. As we look at skills and techniques, examine your own style of managing time and money, and ask yourself whether you really are getting the most out of your resources. Even your greatest assets have to be strengthened for them to serve you best.

TICK TICK TOCK

Our day is divided into many pieces, and depending on our circumstances, we have varying degrees of control over what we do in them. Doctors have appointments to keep, and bus drivers have a schedule to follow. Actors have rehearsals and curtain times, and customer-service reps know that the phone never stops ringing. In theory, we all have eight hours for sleep, eight hours for work, and eight hours of so-called spare time, which is often taken up by routine chores and isn't "spare" at all.

Next are some ways to effectively manage your time.

Make Lists

Engineers and theorists will love this approach. Improvisers will resist it strongly. But if you make a list my way, improvisers, you'll find that it works out pretty well for you. These lists are a function of the accurate thinking principle discussed in Chapter 13.

At the start of your day, make a three-part list of things you need to accomplish. The three categories are as follows:

1. Important and Urgent
2. Important and Not Urgent
3. Useful

Divide the things you know you need to do among these categories, and set to work. It may be helpful to create a mental line in your day. Decide to accomplish all the Important and Urgent things by lunch, which leaves the rest of the afternoon for Important and Not Urgent things. While this doesn't always work because of surprises and meetings that take place in the afternoon, it gives a certain structure to things. It also means that you always do more in the course of a day than just put out fires. You wind up with fewer Urgent items because you make sure to attend to things before they are problems.

Improvisers find that this loose schedule still permits them the freedom to attend to most things as inspiration presents itself. Their free-form work habits offer bigger payoffs with time set aside each day for long-term goals. They still have to watch out for distractions: resist the person who wanders into your office with an idle question.

Agree to talk later, and let the opportunity to brainstorm with someone be a reward to yourself for getting the essentials taken care of.

Engineers may find that this arrangement seems too loosely structured to make the day as productive as it could be. If you find that you don't have problems with getting everything done, then don't change your own system. But one thing this approach offers you is reduced maintenance and a smaller investment in a schedule that is, you must admit, a somewhat fragile thing. Filling your day is not the same as using it effectively.

Theorists, the crucial aspect of this approach for you is that line you draw between Urgent and Not Urgent parts of the day. Completing a short list of accomplishments relatively early in the day should get you off and rolling. If it doesn't, don't take your failure to begin as a sign that it's no longer worthwhile even to try. You need to develop the habit of starting.

Plan Some Downtime

Breaks are essential to keeping your mind sharp, allowing your imagination to digest all the information you feed it, and keeping yourself sane. Try to schedule at least two fifteen-minute periods in the course of your workday when you do no work.

Engineers, you have to resist the temptation to regard standing in line to renew your driver's license as relaxation. It's good to make use of this time by reading or contemplating something, but don't think of it as relaxation. Allowing yourself a few breaks in the course of the day keeps you from stressing. Make sure you aren't stinting on your lunches either: sit down someplace, don't try to write a report while eating, and pick food that you can enjoy whenever possible. A couple of fifteen-minute breaks elsewhere in the day will prevent you from exhausting yourself to no good purpose.

Improvisers, you may also find that relaxation comes hard. There's always something calling you, and your free-form schedule encourages other people to try to draw you into their activities. For you, it's best that relaxation breaks occur at the same time every day. You'll derive the same revitalization from downtime that engineers do, but you'll also find that you gain some fresh perspective on what really does need to happen next. Although you tend to be very social people, this relaxation time is best spent alone. Even your best friend can distract you and draw you off into activities that don't really have significance for you.

Theorists, you should not take breaks in the middle of the day. Instead, allot yourself a generous amount of time at the end of the day. Make a pact with yourself that you'll get to take it only if you've made satisfactory progress earlier in the day. You find it much too easy to extend your breaks, and, before you know it, the whole day will have gone by.

Make Predictions

At the beginning of each month, write down on a sheet of paper the major things you want to accomplish over the next thirty or so days. Seal the paper into an envelope, and then, on the last day of the month, open the envelope and look over your goals. Did you accomplish everything? When? Were some things done early, or have you breathlessly managed to finish everything a few hours before?

The first time you do this, you'll get an eye-opening look at how accurate your goal setting is. Maybe you'll discover that as busy as you were all month, even though you have a sense of accomplishing many things, you haven't gotten to what you thought was important. Or you might decide that you've been underestimating yourself. If you hit every item on the list by the fifteenth of the month, it's probably time to begin taking on more tasks. And if you look at the list and see many items that are almost, but not quite, accomplished, you'll know that what you need is that extra bit of diligence to bring your plans to fruition.

As you seal the envelope for the second month's worth of predictions, you'll be challenging yourself to make better use of your time. Don't let that challenge be disruptive. It can be tempting to produce a superhuman list of tasks, but that isn't what making predictions is for. Don't add anything that would tempt you to cut corners or might threaten your larger plan for success. When you open the envelope at the end of the month, you might not be satisfied yet with your productivity, but you'll understand a great deal more about how you're using your time and how you can improve the way you work.

Engineers, you'll want to resist the temptation to use your predictions like a bus schedule. Circumstances change, and you need to remain flexible. If something arises that requires your time and attention, don't

hesitate to adapt to new opportunities and new problems. It's rare that you don't have a clear sense of what
needs to be done and when. For you, the question is
whether you see a plan as a tool or a set of command-
ments. This approach can show you that making adjustments isn't a form of heresy.

Improvisers are most likely to find that some items on
their lists remain month after month. It's not that you
don't know what needs doing, but your struggle is to arrange things so that your free-flowing ways of working
address more than the needs of the moment. More than
engineers or theorists, you'll find that your goals often
take second place to the needs of other people. If you're
the one who's always responding to help someone else
in crisis, you won't be attending to your own needs. Try
to avoid these distractions, and place extra emphasis on
your own goals in the course of the month.

Theorists, you're going to discover that a lingering
sense of deadline helps sharpen your resolve to work as
well as to just plan to work. You may have the biggest
shock when you open your envelope at the end of the
month because you'll see how much remains to be done.
I'd urge you to use this technique over shorter periods,
say every week or two weeks, to heighten your sense of
passing time. You're capable of accomplishing a great
deal, usually in short, panicked bursts, but you can learn
to apply that industry more methodically. Once you begin seeing the fruits of your labor, you'll find that you
don't need to prod yourself into working. You'll work for
the sense of accomplishment.

We all combine some aspects of each of these three styles of time management. We can be engineers when it comes to routine chores, improvisers in family matters, and theorists when it comes to our own major purpose. It's important that you decide which of these styles dominates your work habits and which is holding you back.

Napoleon Hill saw two types of styles: doers and drifters. *Doers*, he wrote, are rare, the two people in a hundred who have a plan for success and are making daily efforts to see it come true. *Drifters*, the vast majority, stick to old habits of just getting by, complaining of being unhappy with life but never making a systematic effort to alter their circumstances.

You're a doer. You wouldn't have read this far without something more than idle curiosity. You know what you want, and you know how to get it. Any sense you have right now that you aren't accomplishing all that you're capable of is simply an indication of how primed you are to become a tremendously effective doer.

Make some predictions now. Stuff an envelope with what you'll accomplish in just one week and get to work. Equipped with your new awareness of what is possible, you'll open that envelope in a week's time and amaze yourself with what you've done. The transition from potential doer to actual doer takes that little time. Once you've made that realization, you'll know that not a month, week, or day has to go by without the thrill of accomplishment that comes from applying your time as you know it needs to be applied.

What are you waiting for?

MONEY

Money is a delightful tool. It's a device we use to accomplish everything from feeding and clothing ourselves to creating a sense of security and insulation from life's nasty surprises. We all need it to some degree or another, but no matter whether you require freight cars of it or just enough to keep a roof over your head, controlling how you spend and acquire it is vital. It's important to look things over to make certain that you're using your money to further your goals. It's easy to get into a money rut, spending on what you've always spent on, simply because you've found a comfortable pattern. Ask yourself how old this pattern is. Does it date from a time before you knew what you wanted in life? Does it take your major purpose into account? Maybe it's time to reevaluate what has worked before to find out if something can work better.

The advice that follows will be directed at people who find that money is a struggle for them. But even financial moguls won't suffer for looking over their budgets and asking some of the same hard questions. It's important that your money goes to the things that are most significant to you.

Savings

A convenient rule of thumb says that you should set aside 10 percent of your monthly earnings and that you should have an emergency fund big enough to live on for three months. These benchmarks are most suitable for people on a fixed salary. Freelancers and people involved in seasonal businesses know that lean times follow fat, and they should adjust accordingly.

Saving money seems impossible when you're struggling financially. But it's essential, not simply for your long-term financial health, but because having a cushion reduces the fear of being impoverished. If you feel financially panicked, you're going to make bad decisions for the sake of a moment's respite.

If you're not saving regularly, begin now. Set aside something every week, even a sum as small as $20, which would give you $1,040 plus interest a year from now. (Does that sound like an amazing amount of money to have? Then you really need to be saving.) Successful saving is a habit, and it only grows stronger the longer you stick to it. Transfer the money into a savings account; don't simply earmark it in your checking account as not to be spent, because you'll spend it.

The money you save weekly has to come first, before anything else. It's far easier to stretch the money for other things than it is to try to find the money to save after you've done your spending. If you have a payroll deduction plan at work, use that. If not, transfer money into your savings account the day your paycheck goes in. Start thinking of your paycheck in terms of its value after you've made your savings deduction. Don't tempt yourself into counting that extra money even toward paying the bills.

After you save for a short time, you'll be excited. If you've been living from paycheck to paycheck, having a cushion is astoundingly gratifying. Concentrate your sense of accomplishment on what you now know is possible by increasing your savings contribution. There is no better way to feel that you're mastering money than to see the balance in one account go up dependably.

> **There is no better way to feel that you're mastering money than to see the balance in one account go up dependably.**

Eventually, you'll reach the point where you're making a significant savings contribution each month and have a sufficient rainy day fund to cover your needs in an emergency. This is the point at which you can begin to explore other options, including retirement planning and investing in the stock market. Don't put your rainy day money any place where it will cost you a penalty to access it, and don't invest it in anything that carries a risk. There is an enormous temptation to try to make money with your first significant savings, but resist it. You need to know that money is always there for you. Wise investment can be very profitable, but you should never, ever buy stocks or mutual funds with money that you can't afford to lose.

> **All smart investors are also savers.**

Making the transition from saver to investor can be exciting, but it should be done carefully. Seek advice, begin small and carefully, and always remember that investment carries the risk of loss. All smart investors are also savers.

Budgeting

Writing out a budget is an amazingly revealing activity because it can show you how much money is being spent without a worthwhile purpose. Working from your checkbook and credit card statements will give you the broad outlines of where your money goes. Categorize your expenses, and find out what you're spending on the mortgage or rent, food, clothing, and utilities, as well as entertainment, transportation, and medical bills. You'll discover two important things: (1) a good deal of money is still unaccounted for as there are little cash expenditures for everything from coffee to impulse buys; and (2) you'll be shocked at how high a percentage is being spent on things you never planned to buy.

A certain amount of flexible spending isn't a bad thing, for example, flowers to celebrate good news. But as soon as you're aware of how quickly money flows out for items like this, you'll begin becoming more deliberate and more frugal about them. It's these little expenses that can add up in a month and put the pinch on you. They are the easiest places to economize in your spending.

Other family members will probably resist. You'll overcome their resistance best by making sure they know that you're as much a "victim" of your own thriftiness as they are, and by giving them a sense of the purpose behind your choices. There's nothing wrong with explaining that money can only be spent once, either on new sneakers or a family vacation, or that the roof needs to be reshingled this month, and other things take a back seat. Teaching children about how you choose to spend money is a great way to give them a good awareness of the value of money long before they are earning and spending their own.

Beware of false economies. Cheap things that wear out fast are more expensive than more costly well-made items. If you decide you're going to take lunch to work all week and buy groceries accordingly, make sure you allot the time to make those lunches or the food may go to waste. If you decide to save money by doing something yourself that someone else would normally do, whether it's mowing the lawn or washing the car, it's a fair question whether your time isn't more valuably spent on some other activity.

The first look at your budget can be shocking. Avoid the temptation to make huge changes immediately. Rather, be methodical and observant about the effects of your new approach. Spending habits can be changed, but doing so takes effort and can be accomplished best through focused endeavor. If you tackle things hurriedly, you'll only frustrate yourself and decide that it was all a waste of time.

Remember that a budget is a tool, not a law. Allocate money according to your needs and priorities, not percentages that work for others. Your job may require expensive clothes or a good deal of driving, which brings along high gas and car-maintenance costs. A monthly family outing can be worth every penny if it strengthens bonds.

Just work to be sure that you know why you're spending what you are. Awareness alone is a great money saver. You'll quickly come to understand how every dollar that goes out is either serving your interests or thwarting them.

Making adjustments to the ways you spend time and money is a perpetual process. There's nothing wrong with recognizing that something needs to change because it doesn't do the job it once did. The key to effective resource management is a willingness to adapt, combined with an awareness of your goals and the determination to make necessary changes.

Your plan for achieving your major purpose will be your guide in allocating the time and money at your disposal. It will allow you to foresee needs before they arise, and it will provide you with a basis for making decisions, even choosing to make sacrifices when they are necessary. As you come to understand your particular needs and abilities, it can be appropriate to adjust your plan accordingly, but please don't make the mistake of underestimating what you're capable of doing.

As with all the principles of success, you'll grow enormously in your ability to manage your resources. You'll find that acting on faith in your ability to succeed is an important part of using time and money fruitfully. Don't dwell too much on the idea of limitation. Focus your thinking on effectiveness, not scarcity, as you implement your plan. Though both time and money may be in short supply as you start out, you can make them abundant through your conscious efforts to achieve your major purpose.

Chapter 16

Living Smart

"Learn the difference between being smart and wise and you will have more knowledge than many who believe they are highly educated."

—Napoleon Hill

As you grow more confident in your ability to succeed, and as you add more challenges and responsibilities to your life, the importance of your major purpose will grow even larger and stronger than it is now. Proving to yourself that you're a successful person is a powerful experience. People who can channel that new sense of power into constructive action begin to feel more alive than they ever have, and they take more satisfaction from their daily activities than they once believed was possible.

Your sense of possibility, your knowledge that you've taken control of the course of your life, is one of the great rewards of Napoleon Hill's ideas. Like many people, you may discover that this realization is as valuable to you as anything else you learn from Hill's philosophy. Long before you finally achieve your great ambition, you'll feel strong, successful, and proud of yourself and your life.

In the midst of this heady excitement, you may also feel the pull to concentrate all your energy, all your effort, and all your time on your plan for success. There's nothing wrong with this; in fact, it's most likely necessary. The greater your ambitions, the more of yourself you'll have to offer to achieve them. But in doing so, don't sacrifice your mental and physical health.

Staying healthy is a constant refrain in the media today. As previously noted, there are untold numbers of magazines and websites devoted to the subject; newspapers and television run regular features on fitness and diet and disease. If you took all the information available as gospel, you'd be paralyzed because much of it is contradictory. You'd also be an emotional wreck, as the theme behind most reports is "pay attention to this information or you'll suffer."

Ignore these fads, but do pay attention to your health because a strong mind and body are useful in achieving your major purpose, but even more essential to savoring your successes in both the long and short term. Your health, like every other principle of success, can't be left to its own devices. It requires attention and action. Once again, the most important factor in your efforts to stay healthy is your attitude.

PMA = HMA

A Positive Mental Attitude equals a Healthy Mental Attitude. PMA helps you act to keep yourself healthy, and it keeps your mind focused on healthy thoughts. You can wear yourself down and make yourself sick either by deed or by thought. Keeping your mind positive guards against both.

There is little dispute about what keeps us healthy. Regular exercise keeps your body toned and your heart strong. Plenty of sleep helps you stay alert and energetic. It's important to pay attention to routine. All these issues are important to staying healthy. But if you approach them as chores, as tasks that have been assigned to you by medical authorities, they will always remain unpleasant. At best, you'll perform them dutifully, and that's where PMA can play an important role.

When you approach these caretaking tasks with full awareness of what you're getting out of them, you'll find that they seem less onerous. Exercise isn't a constant battle to stay slender: it's a way of pumping energy through your body. Sleep isn't something you collapse into at the end of a long day: it's a time of recharging and revitalizing. And since you know that your imagination and subconscious will continue to work for you while you slumber, you don't have to succumb to the idea that sleep is somehow time taken away from reaching your goals.

Staying healthy is a habit, just like all the other actions that put the principles of success to work for you. If you approach the small, routine things that ensure good health with a conviction that you're benefiting from them—instead of thinking of them as things that must be done—you'll find that these habits become quickly entrenched. They'll be automatic, you won't dread them, and you'll do them very willingly.

As you alter your thinking so that you know you're taking care of yourself, you'll discover that your sense of yourself as a healthy person will grow. New decisions about your health will become easier to make.

PMA won't prevent cancer or even a common cold. There are no guarantees that doing everything right will stop random problems of any sort. But what PMA will do is prepare you to cope with illness if it comes.

The attitude with which you approach a grave illness or a three-day flu has a profound effect on your ability to recover and to continue to define your life on your own terms. If your health requires it, you may need to marshal every resource you possess in an effort to get well. But without PMA, you'll approach that battle with a sense of looming defeat. You won't tap all the assets you need; you won't fight as hard as you must; and you'll spend as much time battling despair as battling your condition.

If, on the other hand, you do have PMA, you'll be able to fight the good fight and win. You'll seek information and become an active participant in your treatment. Your own attitude will affect everyone you depend on for getting well. Doctors and nurses may even be able to do more for you because you have it in you to do what it takes. Family and friends will rally for you, inspired by your resolve.

Paying attention to your health, with a focus on the idea that you're doing what it takes to keep yourself well, is the essence of a healthy mental attitude, so it's important that you seek out doctors and other professionals who support this idea. Someone who won't explain a procedure to you, or who does it condescendingly or impatiently, isn't helping to keep you well. Ask questions freely, seek second opinions, and, if necessary, find a new health-care provider who understands just how significant a role you have to play in your own wellness.

PHYSICAL WELLNESS

Here are some factors that have a bearing on your ability to create success for yourself.

Weight and Exercise

Weight has a significant impact on health. People who are significantly overweight have increased chances of many diseases and live shorter lives. That said, it isn't as significant that you fit neatly into someone's conception of your ideal weight. A slender person who gets no exercise is worse off in my book than a heavy person who regularly exercises. Why?

To begin, cardiac fitness is as significant a factor in health as weight. Three or four sessions a week of vigorous exercise may not melt off the pounds, but it has other benefits:

1. Your heart is stronger and so are the muscles you use.
2. Regular exercise increases your energy levels.
3. You create a habit of doing something healthy, which is always good.
4. The positive habit of exercising is more likely to lead you to do something else good for your health than a negative habit of avoiding food.

None of these are excuses for failing to deal with serious weight issues, especially those which are having a noticeable impact on your health. But you'll be much better off making a realistic change in your behavior than doing something drastic, such as following a fad diet. If your weight goes up and down because you follow a strict regimen for a short time then go back to old habits, you're just telling yourself that it's okay to gain weight because you can lose it again. This is both a mental message and a physical one. Starving yourself, then eating heavily, tells your body that food comes in cycles of abundance and scarcity. Your body will add fat accordingly when it can, as insurance against those times of scarcity.

Your weight is something that you need to deal with on your own terms, for your own reasons. Dieting to be attractive to others will never last, if for no other reason than that you'll never be attractive to everyone. You'll still experience rejection, no matter what you weigh, and if your whole motivation for losing weight is to be universally attractive, you'll soon decide that you've failed, and give up.

Consider your weight in terms of a broader picture of how healthy you can be. If you've got ten pounds that never seem to disappear, maybe it doesn't really have to. Maybe it's time to evaluate your overall fitness, rather than the size of your belly.

Smoking

An astonishing number of people still smoke. If you're a smoker, you don't need a lecture about all the problems you're setting yourself up for. But when you're ready to quit, you have an array of talents and techniques at your disposal that you've learned from this book. You know how to replace a bad habit with a good one. You know how to apply self-discipline, how to use your enthusiasm to motivate yourself, and how to create PMA to achieve things that are important to you.

Stopping smoking will save you money. It will keep your clothes and your house from smelling. It will demonstrate to other people that you're capable of making significant, hard choices because giving up cigarettes is hard. It will provide you more energy, improve your dental health, and give you the satisfaction of an important accomplishment.

Intoxicants

You don't have to be an alcoholic to realize that alcohol plays too big a role in your life. And you don't have to be a drug addict to use drugs to gloss over other issues that you need to deal with.

A glass of wine with a good dinner or a cold beer at a barbecue are fine. The real issue is whether you use any substance as a way of helping yourself avoid something. The best test is to see what happens if you decide to forgo that drink the next time you think about partaking. If you're still feeling the urge half an hour later, then maybe you need to think long and hard about why you're using alcohol.

Sometimes it's purely a matter of habit: you always have a drink when you go out to dinner. Realize this, and you can probably break the habit and soon find that you're only indulging when a special occasion calls for it.

But if you can't really shake the habit, then it's time to seek help. Most likely, your usage is still at an early stage and hasn't begun to cause problems, or you wouldn't need this chapter to point this out. But it will cause spiraling problems if you refuse to deal with it, so find a counselor or a support group, and make a commitment to stopping.

MENTAL WELLNESS

Your mind is yours to control. All the principles you've learned in this book and begun to apply are enormously beneficial to your mental health: they give you a sense of strength and security, help you achieve clarity in your thinking, and focus your mental energies on creating things that are positive and rewarding.

But that doesn't mean that you shouldn't seek help when you need it. Seeking support and guidance to deal with emotional troubles is as wise and positive a step as adopting PMA. It's nothing more than forming a Master Mind alliance for the purpose of keeping your mind healthy.

You're not weak or incompetent because you seek advice from a therapist or a support group. The real weakness would be in denying that you need help from outside, and this applies whether you're just beginning to achieve what you want in life or you're so close to your goal that you can taste it. Depression and addictions aren't signs of failure. They don't indicate bad character, a lack of intelligence, or a paucity of talent.

While you're working to overcome an issue, you can still be making progress toward your major purpose. The satisfaction you derive from your work can be an important tool in restoring your sense of equilibrium and freedom. Don't feel you have to be perfect: you only need to be confident that you're doing what is necessary.

All the principles in this book will be enormously helpful to you in keeping your mind healthy. An active imagination, a subconscious that is directed to positive thoughts, a sense of capability and accomplishment, and control over your habits are all central to keeping your **You can make yourself healthier tomorrow than you are today, simply by deciding that's what you want.** mental outlook strong and vital. Some of your most powerful mental faculties, especially imagination, often do their best work when they are stimulated in some completely new way. If you're always on task, you won't ever give your mind the freedom to work on its own. In a life that's full of pressure, it can be good to turn to something satisfying that has nothing whatsoever to do with your career or any other ambition.

Grab that brass ring with pleasure and the knowledge that you'll be able to enjoy it for as long as possible, and your victory in life will be even sweeter.

You can make yourself healthier tomorrow than you are today, simply by deciding that's what you want. You do have to work at it, and the work isn't always fun, but the rewards are great.

Good health helps create success, but far more important, it makes it possible to enjoy success whenever and wherever you create it.

Chapter 17

Making the Great Connection

"These seventeen principles are the essence of the action and attitude of everyone who has ever had a lasting accomplishment."

—W. Clement Stone

I do hope that every one of Napoleon Hill's principles discussed in this book is becoming a part of your life. Your odds of attaining your major purpose will be much smaller if you ignore any of the lessons in this book. Yet, what is most important about Napoleon Hill's ideas isn't that there are a certain number of discrete principles, but that they each reflect on and relate to the others. You can't really implement one without at least a few of the others.

Each principle of success is, in a way, simply an aspect of this last principle. Napoleon Hill called it Cosmic Habitforce. You could also call it *Connectivity*. Simply put, it says that all your thoughts and actions create the world in which you live. Your hopes and fears, dreams, and deeds determine what happens to you. We came closest to touching on this idea in the lessons on applied faith and going the extra mile, when we dealt with preparing yourself for opportunity and success. But this principle is so overarching and so profound in its implications that it bears examination on its own.

You've probably encountered variations on this theme in other ways. Some people call it living by the Golden Rule. Others think of it as karma, though I'm not talking about what happens to you in another lifetime. Connectivity is at the heart of Napoleon Hill's maxim: whatever you can conceive and believe, you can achieve.

Are you ready to start thinking about your life as a way of preparing yourself for success? The idea is liberating and disturbing at the same time. It gives you freedom and responsibility in equally enormous portions. The results are not always neatly, precisely predictable: this can be both thrilling and shocking. But embracing Connectivity is the one sure way to unite all the other principles of success so that every one of them works for you in attaining your major purpose.

UNIVERSAL TRUTH

The universe works in fixed, undeniable ways, and you need to understand these truths to succeed in getting what you want out of life.

First and most important, for every action there is a re-action. Nothing you do happens in a void. Even something as simple as breathing creates a complicated series of reactions in your lungs, bloodstream, and muscles. At the same time, you alter the content of the air in your room, removing oxygen, expelling carbon dioxide and water, disturbing the existing currents of air, raising the temperature ever so slightly. Every breath you take literally alters the world, and nothing else you do is without effect either.

Second, nothing happens without a cause. There are random events, so the chaos theorists tell us, but even randomness happens in response to a stimulus. Randomness is a question of causes we can't fully understand or predict, not of spontaneous, arbitrary changes. Predicting how your exhaled breath will alter the weather patterns in your town is impossible because so many random results are possible from even that small action. But the weather, as complicated as it is and as hard as it is for us to understand, happens because of a multitude of causes. It doesn't simply happen out of nowhere, no matter how it may seem to you when it rains a day after glorious sunshine.

Third, you can't create something from nothing. Matter can be converted to energy and vice versa. But any change in the world, whether in the shape or location of matter, or the kind or intensity of energy, requires that something be given up. Nothing springs into existence on its own: everything that exists is the result of an interaction between other existing forces and objects. Even the supposedly "free" energy we harness in solar collectors is the result of complex fusion reactions in the sun, and the collection process itself demands the creation of specific objects, which requires the investment of matter and energy themselves before they can begin to harvest energy from the sky.

These first three ideas are scientific commonplaces that you may remember from high school chemistry and physics courses. Millions of people know them. The real question is whether they ever think to apply them and, in applying them, begin to shape their lives. The vast majority of people simply fail to recognize the fourth and final universal truth:

You're as much a part of these physical systems as an atom beneath the crust of Pluto, with one crucial difference. You have the ability to choose how you act and how you react, for what cause, and what you'll use to create the things you want.

You're a human being. As far as we know, humans are unique in the universe for our ability to determine a purpose for our existence and choose how we'll fulfill that purpose. (And even if there are other creatures out among the stars with a similar gift, it's that gift that will define them in the same way it defines us.)

The whole purpose of Napoleon Hill's philosophy is to awaken you to this realization. You can shape your life through the use of these universal truths. If you don't make this realization, you'll still be subject to these truths, but they, not you, will completely define who you are. You'll be as much at the mercy of the great forces of the world as a solar particle screaming past the Earth into trillions of years of cold oblivion, on its way to becoming the detritus of the galaxy, useless, forgotten, and ultimately alone.

But if you do awaken to the idea that you're not simply an atom expelled from a vast and complex reaction, you can become anything you want. You'll then choose to devote your thinking and your actions to shaping the way the universe responds to you. Though they are significant, the truths you must acknowledge are infinitely flexible. You'll find your own way of applying them, and from that application, you'll attain your major purpose.

ACTION AND REACTION

Up until now, you've probably spent your life reacting. You've responded to ideas and images, songs and stories, and physical urges. But by applying what you've learned from this book, you've started to alter the equation. No longer are you simply an object—you're a force.

You've decided what your major purpose is by now, making your choice freely, out of your own wishes, not to fulfill the expectations of family and society. In making that choice on your own, you were stepping back for a moment from simply responding to life, and realizing that you could shape it.

> **There is simply no better guarantee that your actions will produce desirable results than to keep your thinking positive and constructive.**

You're continually making choices. You can't know the long-term effects of every action. Randomness will bring surprises, good and bad. But sustained, deliberate actions—in the long run—will produce systematic, consistent results. And the question therefore becomes, what sort of choices are you making?

This is why this book began with PMA. There is simply no better guarantee that your actions will produce desirable results than to keep your thinking positive and constructive. If your actions are predicated on fears of failure, on the expectation of disappointment, then those are the results you'll eventually reap. If your actions are based, instead, on belief in success, then success is what you'll wind up with.

The same is true of your thinking, only more so. Action takes time, and we can only do so many things at once. But thoughts! We can have thoughts in an instant, hundreds of them in the time it takes to put on a pair of shoes. The thoughts you think have reactions just as assuredly as your deeds do. PMA is the best, surest way to make your thoughts produce the reactions you want in life.

Don't trouble yourself about occasional doubts, flashes of anger or jealousy, or other fleeting negative emotions. If you cultivate PMA relentlessly—yes, relentlessly—you'll overbalance the snippets of negative thinking. But if you do detect regular, habitual negative thinking, then redouble your efforts to build PMA.

Universal truths won't invariably punish you for past negative thinking if you devote yourself to strong positive thoughts now. Sometimes, though, you may have to cope with a negative event set in motion long ago. Don't delay. Acknowledge the role you played; make amends swiftly and generously; and never, ever, sit there wondering what negative event will visit you next. Worry breeds worry. Honest responses, however, go a very long way to defusing old errors. It may very well be that admitting one old negative deed or thought frees you from facing more. And if it doesn't, remember that the sooner you accept responsibility, the sooner you'll be adding that positive action to your store of helpful, constructive effects on the world.

In Chapter 11, Living a Value-Added Life, you saw how you can prepare yourself for unexpected benefits by being liberal in dispensing them to others. When these wonderful things come your way, acknowledge them openly, share them whenever possible, and never stop to tally in your head whether you're finally getting back more than you gave. It doesn't matter whether you ever do. Giving up your seat on a bus to someone who needs it doesn't guarantee that someday, someone will do the same for you. The universe is just not that tidy. And you don't want it to be. You may never need a bus seat. The help you need at an important moment will likely be wholly different.

What is important is that you get what you want and need for your major purpose. Accept and celebrate the good reactions you've created for yourself; in doing so, you'll only prepare yourself for more.

What goes around, comes around. Be generous, receive generosity. Be positive, receive positive energy back. Be stingy. . . .

CREATING A CAUSE

Deciding on a purpose for your life means that you start determining the cause of events in your life. You won't be the only cause, but you can become the dominating cause, creating a tide of events and circumstances that brings you to where you need to be in order to be happiest. Make

a daily effort to remind yourself of what is most important to you. Concentrating all your thoughts on your goal
for even a few minutes a day will alter the color of everything you do that day. It won't blind you to the needs of
other people, but it will ensure that even the most routine
tasks and chores are undertaken with a sense of how they
can help you attain your major purpose.

One of the disturbing consequences of learning the
principles of success is that you come to realize how
seemingly trivial actions affect your progress toward
what you want: a handshake, the closing of a letter, the
bag of potato chips you eat at lunch, or the article you
read in a magazine. All of these have effects on yourself,
your relationships with others, and your major purpose.
It's easy to feel overwhelmed by this realization. But the
surest way to counteract your sense of enormous responsibility is to make certain that your mind is fixed on what
you want in life.

Accurate thinking and controlled attention depend
on having a definite purpose, a cause. When they are in-
formed by a keen awareness of your goal in life, small
things don't require agonizing decision-making: you
know automatically what will serve your purpose and
you swiftly act accordingly. Even if you realize later that
at one particular moment, there was a better choice to
be made, you still know that you're accumulating a history of deeds and actions that bring you closer to your
goal.

Perfection is impossible in human beings because our
imaginations can always devise a better way of being and

doing. What you're striving for in creating Connectivity isn't an absolute, crystal-clear purity, but an ever-building movement toward the self you've decided to become. Mistakes and failures will occur, but with the knowledge that the force of your life is directed toward a worthy goal, you'll understand how even a temporary setback has some value to you. Your enthusiasm will survive temporary failure and disappointment as long as you retain your momentum toward your objective.

There will be events that are baffling to you. Randomness is the name we give to causes so intricate that we can't immediately unravel them. But randomness will be less threatening and seem far less arbitrary when you have the conviction that you are in pursuit of a just cause. You'll know that the shape and direction of your life are still defined by your major purpose, and that knowledge will provide you with the resolve, energy, and resourcefulness you need to deal with anything unforeseen.

What is equally important, though, is that becoming the shaper of your own destiny means that the vast majority of circumstances and events start to reflect your own needs and wants. You'll become successful. Breaks will go your way. You'll be someone who finds what you need in the world. Others may call you lucky, but you'll know that you've created your own luck by understanding and using a universal truth.

Success, they say, breeds success. This isn't really as true as the idea that success arises from a number of actions and thoughts that, having made one goal possible, make even more goals attainable. Become the dominating cause in your life, and you'll create for yourself the same kind of momentum.

SOMETHING FOR SOMETHING

Earlier, we addressed how you would react if you suddenly found yourself penniless and owning nothing more than the clothes on your back. The point was to help you realize that the most valuable thing you'll ever possess is your mind, not stocks or an SUV, or even knowledge, respect, or skills.

From your mind, anything else can spring. Your mind can create anything you need for reaching your goal. This doesn't mean that you can simply will something into existence, but that your mind, properly directed, can discover the means by which an object, a mood, or a state of being can be created or attained. An active mind leads to action, which must occur if you are to achieve your definite major purpose.

The route to getting what you want will involve a series of exchanges. You'll likely exchange labor and time for money, and you'll exchange money for objects that will allow you to labor better, and, in turn, acquire learning, transportation, food, goods, communication, and anything else you need, to wind up with that thing you envisioned.

Your major purpose is gained only by offering something else in return. In essence, you exchange things that are less valuable to you for things that are more valuable, and you repeat this process over and over. As a member of a consumer society, this probably seems very evident to you in some ways. You know you need cash to buy a cell phone or a pair of shoes.

But the hard truth is that it's easy to forget this fundamental idea when it comes to a long-term purpose. There are always everyday needs that place a drain on your resources, and even when money isn't tight, time isn't dispensed like stock options or yearly bonuses. Great Aunt Harriet may leave you a thousand shares of Berkshire Hathaway, but there's no way that she'll manage to will you an extra hour a day for the next fifty years.

So, it's up to you to make certain that you're always putting out more than just what you need back today. Sometimes, the immediate rewards will be so satisfying that you won't have any difficulty with this. But we all face situations when something is required of us that isn't satisfying. It could be attention to tax-filing details, to writing reports, to learning a new skill, or to getting a professional certification. You have to approach these tasks with a sense of giving them your best effort, just as you do the things that you enjoy about your life and work.

It should go without saying that you must always remain honest and fair in everything you do. Any exchange built on deceptions or tricks will quickly fall apart, and you'll find that you wind up with much less than you thought you were getting by pulling a fast one. Worse, you'll begin expecting dishonesty from other people, and you'll find out that they reward you with it many times over. The momentum of your life will carry you toward further deceptions and betrayals, and, even if, for some brief moment, you achieve your major purpose, it will evaporate in your hands, as much an illusion as the fabrications you used to create it.

If what you offer in exchange for what you want is shoddy and unreliable, you'll also be paid back in things that are shoddy and unreliable. On the other hand, if what you offer is good and solid and honest, then that is what you'll receive in return.

COSMIC HABITFORCE

Napoleon Hill used the phrase Cosmic Habitforce because it embodies the idea that everyday actions have a cumulative effect of enormous power. It can seem unrealistic to imagine that when you use self-discipline to tackle a routine chore, you're activating a huge vortex of power that shifts the action of the universe in your favor, but that is really what happens.

Each time you read your statement of purpose, you alter the world. Each time you go the extra mile, the galactic dynamic shifts. The changes occur on a macrocosmic level, altering what you can expect to come back to you from the actions of others, and they occur on a microcosmic level, inside you. The world becomes more disposed to respond to you in accordance with your purpose in life, and you become more disposed to act in accordance with your purpose in life.

Yes, success is built of small things as well as great visions. If you had to wrench your mind around to paying attention to every single detail of your success, and each time you had to act as if all your chances rode on that detail—from the crease in your pants to the place-ment of a postage stamp—either your mind would ex-plode or you would collapse from exhaustion before breakfast.

Instead, Cosmic Habitforce allows you to build mo-mentum. By providing yourself with a direction and by creating habits and routines that you know work in your favor, you can make your choices more swiftly; be confi-dent that they are supporting your efforts; and expend your energies on the more crucial, big picture issues.

This doesn't mean that you work any less hard, but it does mean that your work is going to the construction, rather than just to the maintenance, of your major pur-pose. You make a transition from holding your own to moving ahead. You gain the ability to grow and learn, and you exchange a dreary routine for an exciting sense of new frontiers and new challenges.

Even if you close this book and never open it again, Napoleon Hill's ideas will have entered your mind, and you'll find yourself applying them. You'll get more done, have more respect for yourself, and feel better about what you accomplish.

Commit yourself to putting Napoleon Hill's ideas into practice. It all begins with determining what you want from life, and from there, you'll have made the first, most important step toward achieving your major purpose because, at that moment, you begin altering the world around you.

Make the commitment to yourself, and the universe, through Cosmic Habitforce or Connectivity, that you'll begin to change in accordance with your purpose. All the other principles in this book are simply the means for increasing your power over the actions of yourself and those in your universe. You are *that* powerful. You can make every single change in yourself that needs to be made and thereby change the world around you.

Remember:

Whatever your mind can conceive and believe, it can achieve.

Index